MW00737283

Lakota Grieving

A Pastoral Response

Stephen Huffstetter, SCJ

TIPI PRESS

St. Joseph's Indian School
Chamberlain, SD 57326

© 1998

Printed by Tipi Press Printing

Copyright © 1998 by Stephen Huffstetter, SCJ
Published by Tipi Press, St. Joseph's Indian School
Printed by Tipi Press Printing, St. Joseph's Indian School
Manufactured in the United States of America. All rights
reserved.
Reproduction or translation of any part of this work without
written permission of the copyright owner is unlawful.

Cover art by Daniel Long Soldier
Copyright © 1998 by St. Joseph's Indian School

ISBN 1-877976-20-2
Library of Congress Catalog Card Number: 98-60116

Dedicated to the four circles I know as family:

The Huffstetter - Ansboury - Greskowiak - Kesl clans

My SCJ community

My colleagues at Catholic Theological Union

The Cheyenne River Lakota Oyate

Mitakuye Oyasin
(All My Relatives)

Acknowledgement

Thanks to the following people for helping with interviews information and support: Robert Aberle, Rosie Roach Avery, Campion Breske SCJ, Ethel and Oliver Brown Wolf, Rev. Richard Charging Eagle, Debbie Day, Suzie Eagle Staff, Tom Eagle Staff, Carolyn Eultgen SCJ, Iyonne Garreau, John Hatcher SCJ, James Hoerter, Doris Hump, Edie Jewett, Louis Jewett, Austin Keith, J. D. Kessling, Jan, Johnny Klingler SCJ, Ted and Peggy Knife, Gary Lantz SCJ, Mona Lawrence, Monica Lawrence, Chuck LeCompte, Judy Lemke, Eileen Peacock, Frank Presto SCJ, Mert Pritzkau, Olivia Scully PBVM, Yvon Sheehy SCJ, Elsie Slides Off, Jim Walters SCJ, Marty Ward, Tater Ward, Reuben and Doris Ward, Doug Watson SCJ, Jane Weeks, Tom Westhoven SCJ, and Darlene Young Bear. There were also others I talked to more informally along the way, and for all your insights and shared wisdom, I am grateful.

Thanks to the members of my thesis project board, who gave me guidelines and pointed me in the right direction before and during the writing: Claude Marie Barbour, Dianne Bergant CSA, Gerard Goldman, and David Lafferty.

Thanks to my local SCJ community who hung in there during the writing times while I was difficult to live with.

A big thanks to my project director, Herbert Anderson, for the support and direction. Herbert kept affirming my pastoral Heart of a Shepherd, while pushing me to think more critically and systematically like a theologian.

Table of Contents

List of Abbreviations

BIA - Bureau of Indian Affairs
CDW - Congregation for Divine Worship
CRST - Cheyenne River Sioux Tribe
GIRM - General Instruction of the Roman Missal
GS - Gaudium et Spes
ICEL - International Commission on English in the Liturgy
IHS - Indian Health Services
LITF - Lakota Inculturation Task Force, Diocese of Rapid City, SD
OCF - Order of Christian Funerals
PHS - Public Health Services
USDHHS - United States Department of Health and Human Services
YPLL - Years of Potential Life Lost, per 100,000 population

Abstract

At This Time . . . Lakota Grieving: A Pastoral Response explores the grieving practices and rituals of Lakota Catholics on the Cheyenne River Sioux Reservation in South Dakota. The author proposes that Lakota people have taken rituals from both their Lakota and Christian traditions and created a merged culture to meet their grieving needs. Ethnographic interviews with the Lakota provide an overview of current grieving practices on the reservation. Lakota cultural resources that facilitate good grieving and the ways Lakota people can get stuck in their grieving are explored. The interviews and mortality data show that traumatic deaths, conflicted grieving, and multiple loss complicate grieving. The author offers principles for pastoral ministry to people in grief based on recommendations by Lakota people and from his own pastoral ministry among them.

Introduction

When Lakota people gather together, whether it is for a funeral, a pow wow, or most any event, some member of the community, usually an elder, assumes the role as announcer or Master of Ceremonies. At this time . . . is an often heard phrase which prepares the assembly for a change in ritual activity and introduces the next movement.

This thesis project represents the next movement in my own theology and practice of ministry. I worked for almost ten years with Lakota people on the Cheyenne River Sioux Reservation[1] in North Central South Dakota. In three separate assignments from 1980 until 1995, I served as a summer intern, pastoral minister, deacon and parish priest for the ten Roman Catholic parishes. Pastoral ministry to grieving people became a significant focus of that work. When we did a series of town hall type meetings in the parishes the number one religious concern people raised was to encourage working together to take better care of the church's cemeteries.

Before I arrived in South Dakota I took courses on cross cultural ministry, but there was still an adjustment period from culture shock when I moved to the reservation and began ministry. The differences from my culture were most noticeable at times and events connected with death. Wakes were great communal events with story telling and feasting lasting far into the night. Children were not sheltered from the dying but kept vigil with them. At funerals children approached the coffin to see, touch, or talk to the dead. Family members carried their own shovels to the cemetery and buried the coffin themselves. After the funeral, the family gave away treasured possessions of the one who had died. On memorial days families would decorate the graves with food, then gather around for a picnic.

Growing up in a small town in Northern Indiana, I only remember one death of someone who was not elderly. Having to be with people regularly facing the deaths of children and young adults was a new pastoral challenge. Caring for people after many of the alcohol related deaths meant working with survivors often overwhelmed by unresolved

---

[1]"Sioux" comes from an enemy's name for the tribe. The people call themselves Lakota. The reservation itself is locally referred to as Cheyenne River, which is the abbreviated form that will be used throughout this document.

feelings of anger toward the dead. What kind of ministry was appropriate in these situations? When people spoke openly about their experiences of ghosts and spirits, which did not fit my world view, that raised questions about how to respond appropriately.

I tried, often by trial and error, to develop approaches to ministry that addressed these needs. I read what I could, but found no books that adequately, or even specifically, addressed pastoral ministry to grieving Lakota persons. I tried to piece together information and suggestions from many different fields to come up with my own conclusions. I began asking parishioners what comforted or helped them at this time of death. I asked co-workers what practices seemed effective and what did not. My non-Lakota colleagues found that the aspects of Lakota culture connected with grieving and death were the area in which they had to make significant cultural adjustment as well.

I engaged in this ongoing process of bringing questions raised from experience into dialogue with questions raised from theory so they might inform and challenge each other. Participating in Catholic Theological Union's Doctor of Ministry program has helped me to name this as practical theology. Engaging in this structured study of practical theology kindled my desire to take another look at how ministry to grieving parishioners might be improved on the Cheyenne River Reservation.

It is important from the beginning to distinguish between the terms grief and grieving. I use grief for the feelings that come with the loss of someone or something close to us. Grieving is what we do with those feelings. Some use the terms mourning and bereavement to describe the processes and actions people undertake in response to loss. Therese Rando (p. 23) defines mourning as the cultural and/or public display of grief through one's behaviors. I use the term grieving to include such behaviors and choices people in grief make.

I view this project as a handbook or source book for pastoral ministry. It could serve as an orientation and overview for non-Lakota pastoral ministers, especially those SCJ's, lay missioners and members of other religious congregations preparing for ministry in the area. A basic appreciation of all that is going on during these times will help ministers develop more effective pastoral strategies, minister with greater care and compassion, and promote a dialogue which enriches Lakota - Christian spirituality.

My second aim in describing the grieving practices of Lakota people is to explore what insights it might contribute to understanding the grieving process in general. Lakota parishioners' examples encouraged me to face death much more directly and to see it as part of the larger circle of life. They also showed that the work of grieving takes time. Lakota practices may speak to the needs of our broader United States culture, which is often accused of minimizing, rushing through, or trying to deny grief altogether. People can benefit from stepping out of life's routines and entering into a substantial and active grieving process.

A third aim of this thesis is to emphasize the importance of serious cross-cultural study. Effective pastoral practice must engage in an ongoing dialogue with an ever dynamic and continually evolving culture. The people whom we minister among can become our teachers when we find ways to tap into their wisdom and insights. If we listen, those we serve will tell us what they need and how to minister to them. Lakota people can model for ministers how to be pastorally present and what grieving processes and rituals are culturally appropriate.

History has shown, however, that many ministers approached reservation work with all the answers rather than questions. Often they would come to minister filled with fervor and solutions for saving the entire reservation, only to get frustrated and burnt out and leave after a year or two. One common question I was asked when I first arrived was, How long will you be here? It takes time to develop trust, just as it takes time to listen to Lakota people's insights and understandings. A basic understanding of Lakota spirituality and culture can help ministers begin on a more solid foundation. I hope this is helpful in that regard.

In part, this project arises out of past failures at dialogue. Not all that many years ago church ministers totally rejected many elements of Lakota culture in the church. A European Catholicism was held up as the proper and only way to be Catholic. In both church and state run boarding schools the express philosophy was, Save the Man by killing the Indian, as expressions of Lakota culture were ridiculed and forbidden.

3

But Lakota culture has survived. Like any culture it is dynamic and has changed and evolved. Many Lakota people have embraced Christianity, but they do not want to give up being Lakota in order to do so. Roman Catholics on Cheyenne River have taken elements from both Lakota and Roman Catholic traditions and wed them together into their own unique expression of faith. Lakota Catholicism is therefore a merged culture. I believe it is significant to reflect on the theology underlying Lakota Catholic practices. These rituals point to beliefs about God and God's action. These rituals teach people how to grieve. These rituals reinforce traditional cultural values, which teach people what it means to be Lakota and what it means to be a Lakota Christian. A fresh look at the rites of the ultimate transition can provide a grounding in social relationships and cultural values that can see people through other transitions.

SOCIO-ECONOMIC AND DEMOGRAPHIC CONTEXT

The Cheyenne River Sioux Reservation is home to four of the seven Lakota bands: *Minneconjou* (Plant Beside the River), *Itazipco* (Without Bows) also called Sans Arc, *Sihasapa* (Blackfeet) and *Oohenonpa* (Two Kettle). The other bands, the *Oglala* on Pine Ridge, the *Sicangu* or Brule on the Rosebud and Lower Brule Reservations, and the *Hunkpapa* of the Standing Rock Reservation have been more studied and are more widely known. Cultural ways and practices do differ on the various reservations, but more is similar than divergent.

Cheyenne River covers two rural counties, Dewey and Ziebach, in North Central South Dakota. The Missouri River forms the eastern border and the Cheyenne River the southern boundary. It is roughly one hundred miles east to west and fifty miles north to south. When the reservation was carved out of the Great Sioux Reservation in 1889 Cheyenne River had 2.7 million acres. In 1909-10 the government again opened much of that land to homesteaders, leading to non-Indian ownership of 47% of the original land. (Economic Development Administration, pp. 555-556)

About one third of the population living within the external boundaries

4

of Cheyenne River is non-Indian. Even before the coming of homesteaders, French trappers and traders who worked along the Missouri River married into the tribe. Over the years intermarriage has been common. Learning about the history and cultural ways of the children and grandchildren of homesteaders and traders is also helpful for anyone working on Cheyenne River, but that is beyond the scope of this work. But it does set up a social context where cultures, ideas and practices from a variety of sources impact and are influenced by one another. Dewey County has 3689 Tribal members in a population of 5523, or 67%. Ziebach County has 1420 Tribal members of 2220, or 64%. Almost as many enrolled tribal members live off the reservation as on it. It is important to keep in mind that they return home regularly for family events, religious and cultural rituals, and usually for burial.

Though far from complete, the data in Appendix One begins to sketch a picture of the socio-economic and demographic characteristics of the reservation. Ziebach County consistently ranks somewhere in the bottom ten counties of per capita income in the United States. In 1980 it was the second lowest. Overall, three of every five tribal members live below the poverty line, and two of every three children. In a state with one of the lowest unemployment rates in the nation (4.3%), the Census Bureau's figure of 27.9% for the reservation seems incredible. Tribal officials know the rate is even higher because government unemployment rates do not include the chronically unemployed who have given up hope and do not bother looking for a job. The local economy has no manufacturing base and is heavily dependent on agriculture and government programs. It ebbs and flows, depending in large part on which programs Washington decides to fund.

One statistic which has increased since the 1990 census is the percentage of households with a telephone. Realizing that the elderly face health emergencies while residing up to ninety miles away from the hospital, the Tribal government provides that all the elderly now have at least local telephone service. But it is useful for a minister to realize that they cannot always call to set up appointments, nor can they assume people can easily travel into town for a meeting or church activity.

Appendix Two, Deaths Per 100,000 Population, and Appendix Three, Years of Potential Life Lost (YPLL), contain statistical measurements of death on the Cheyenne River Reservation. YPLL is used to get a sense of the frequency that premature death for those under 65 occurs in a community. While the overall death rate in many categories might be expected to be higher than the national average in a poor rural area such as a reservation, the rate of death for most of these categories on Cheyenne River is consistently above the average even when compared to the other Indian Health Service Areas. As a result, multiple loss is a common issue people are working through as they grieve. People on Cheyenne River die of alcoholism eight times more often than in the general population and the rate is almost twice that of other IHS areas. Heart disease and cancer are higher than normal. Suicides run four times the national average.

Accidents are a high ranking cause of death. Motor Vehicle Accidents and Unintentional Injuries are about five times the national average. Other Accidents run three to four times the national average. Guns are common, as many people hunt for their food or keep predators like coyotes away from their livestock, and gun accidents are also a reality. Harsh winters may bring tragic cases of people dying of exposure. Some of the deaths by accident may fall into the category which some call sub-intended deaths, i.e., self-destructive behaviors that in a sense are suicidal. Beyond the numbers, some of the first person narratives in Chapter Two paint a more personal picture of survivors coping with such traumatic deaths.

Appendix Four contains a chart with a visual image of the age of death. These statistics are not for Cheyenne River specifically, but for all the Indian Health Service areas in the Aberdeen, South Dakota Service Unit.[2] But it still shows that on the reservations on the Great Plains, death comes at a young age. In the general U.S. population 72% of those born will live past 65, while in the Aberdeen IHS area only 41% do so. Fifteen percent of the deaths occurred for those under the age of 24, as opposed to only four percent in the general population. One in eleven

[2]The data from the 5 year period from 1988 until 1992 showed only a one or two percentage difference in any given age category.

6

will die before their fourteenth birthday. Pastoral ministers need to be prepared not just to bury parents and grandparents, but children and grandchildren.

Aberdeen Area continues to lead the Indian Health Service in infant mortality rates. In the Aberdeen Area, for every one thousand live births, fifteen infants will die before their first birthday. This is almost twice as many infant deaths that occur in the general U.S. population. Only nine infants will die before their first birthday for all IHS areas. (USDHHS, 1996a p. I)

From 1981-1992 the average number of births on Cheyenne River was 192. On average, three infants died each year, or one death in every 64 live births. That rate would be 48 per thousand, or six times the national average.

The life expectancy at birth for persons in the Aberdeen Area IHS is 64.9 years, 11 years lower than the national average. Males have a life expectancy of 60.8 years, compared to 72.3 years for all U.S. males. Females' life expectancy is 69.3 years compared to 79.1 years for all U.S. females. (USDDHS 1996c, p.85)

Besides death there are other losses that may add to the grieving climate. Takini School on the Southwestern corner of the Reservation takes its name (Survivors) because of the many tribal members who had to continue on after their relatives were massacred at Wounded Knee in 1890. Government boarding schools took many students away from their family for nine months of the year. Lakota speaking was strictly punished in those schools.

The United States Government's policy of homesteading and its unilateral appropriation of tribal lands has been a profound experience of loss for the Lakota People. The United States Supreme Court ruled that the United States government illegally seized the Black Hills, which was the western portion of the Great Sioux Reservation. The government has offered some monies, but the Sioux tribes insist that their sacred land cannot be sold. The tribes are engaged in an ongoing legal struggle for a return of those lands. As recently as 1958, when the Army Corps of

Engineers built the series of Hydro Electric Dams along the Missouri River, thousands of acres were submerged, including entire towns, cemeteries and landmarks. So many are still grieving over what has happened to our people, not just in this generation, but in past generations as well . . . grieving over the loss not only of our people, but of our culture and traditions. We are born into this grief. (Rick Two Dogs, in Abrogast, p.315) Looking at charts and statistics about death on Cheyenne River can paint a depressing picture. People do come face to face with death quite often. But I hope this thesis-project also shows that Lakota people have hope and courage and generosity in the midst of their grieving. Maybe their example can offer other grieving people hope as well.

EXPLANATION OF THE METHOD

Practice, theory, practice! was a phrase Catholic Theological Union's instructors emphasized over and over again to help students understand the dynamics of practical theology. Experiences of ministry raise the questions the theory hopefully addresses. Theory raises new questions about past practices of ministry and leads to fresh ways of reflecting on the forces at work within ministerial encounters. Theory is a partner of practice in an ongoing process that is spiral in nature. Theory and practice push each other toward new insight and growth.

My ministry among the Lakota people in South Dakota was spread over three different time periods. I spent a summer on Cheyenne River during college. That gave me an initial feel for the area and raised as many questions as it answered. I took those questions back into the classroom. After two years of theological studies, I returned for a two-year internship as a pastoral minister, where I again tried to put into practice some of what I had learned. When I returned to school I had a new list of questions in need of answering. A deepened awareness of Christian tradition and theory sent me back to South Dakota to begin ordained ministry with yet new approaches. And after seven more years on Cheyenne River I returned to the Doctor of Ministry program at Catholic Theological Union to continue this learning style. My

8

conversation about the integration of Lakota and Christian ways has been a back and forth dialogue spread over many years.

This thesis project attempts to build on this grounding in practical theology, based on my personal observations from participating in ministry and on the experiences of local Lakota people. Classes with an anthropological and ethnographic emphasis raised questions I had never thought to ask people about their culture. Stepping away from the daily routines of parish work gave me a fresh chance to reflect on what I had seen and heard within this culture. As I returned to the reservation for two months this past year to interview people for this project, I asked questions I would not have thought of two years ago.

The writing of this thesis project employs a method developed by James and Evelyn Whitehead. (1995) They describe theological reflection as a conversation between experience, tradition, and culture. In reality the three areas of culture, tradition and experience overlap. They are so not easily separated, though it is important to distinguish them. Employing this method, this thesis project is organized into four chapters.

For the Whiteheads, the first stage of attending demands identifying specific aspects of experience, culture and tradition in order to listen to what each has to say. Chapter One begins with an examination of the ongoing dialogue within the Roman Catholic Church about the issue of inculturation. It then sketches a broad overview of current ritual practices, such as funerals, wakes and memorials, by the Lakota Catholics on Cheyenne River. Some of the descriptions come from parishioners themselves. Other observations come from my own participation during my years of pastoral ministry there. The Whiteheads would call this the voice of experience. Throughout this thesis project the words taken from interviews are in **bold print**. Substantial portions of eleven of the interviews are presented in Chapter Two, but there are selections from other interviews woven throughout this thesis project. All Lakota words are in **bold italics** and a glossary is included as Appendix Five.

Chapter Two involves Lakota parishioners as they recount experiences connected with a loved one's death. This is an attempt to

9

include more voices of experience, but more specifically, to listen to the voice of culture. I interviewed a varied, but representative, group of parishioners to obtain their reflections and insights on issues connected with grieving.

Chapter Three examines the dynamics of grieving. The themes that begin to emerge from the interviews are brought into dialogue with the voice of tradition, specifically with the social sciences and the Christian tradition. This dialogue raises new questions about what a minister needs to know from the traditions to minister authentically in the Lakota cultural context. Conversation for the Whiteheads does not mean a series of three monologues. An image for the interaction among the three poles is a crucible, where each pole pushes the others toward transformation and change. This describes the movement into the asserting stage for the Whiteheads. I wrestle with the inconsistencies and contradictions these voices raise as the critical questions are debated.

Tom Eagle Staff suggests a Lakota metaphor to describe the Whitehead's method - a *tipi*. Three key poles, tradition, experience and culture, form the tripod at the core of the *tipi*. New poles, representing further contributions, beliefs and voices can be strategically added to give the structure additional balance and strength.

The hoped for outcome from a deepened understanding about grieving, leads to the third stage of the method, pastoral response. Chapter Four suggests some contributions Lakota culture and religious beliefs might make in the field of grieving. Possible directions for a renewed praxis of pastoral ministry on the reservation are suggested.

I use this method first of all, because of the way it honors both Lakota culture and Roman Catholic tradition. I am constantly looking for common ground, trying to find ways that Lakota culture and Roman Catholic tradition can enter into a dynamic partnership that is mutually enriching, rather than being at odds with each other. I also use this method because my pastoral bent is toward reconciling differences. One of my limitations is that I tend to de-emphasize areas of conflict. In the stage of asserting, the method challenges me to bring out areas where

10

the different voices push and confront each other.

The strength of the Whitehead's method is that it can be repeated as new people bring their understanding of culture, experience and tradition to the dialogue. The method is rather simple, which I hope encourages those working in such ministry to take the analysis and dialogue regarding Lakota grieving practices further. The Whiteheads hope they have developed a method which enhances ministry, which is the third reason it has been chosen. My primary motivation for undertaking this thesis project is the hope that, ultimately, this dialogue in some way will improve the practice of ministry among Lakota people who also embrace Christianity.

Chapter One

Rituals
of
Grieving

INCULTURATION

The Lakota people have very successfully amalgamated their culture with Christian and modern trends associated with death and grief. (Brokenleg and Middleton, p. 111)

The people of Cheyenne River have taken rituals from both their Lakota and Christian traditions, adapted elements from the U.S. funeral industry and wed them together into their own unique culture. Attempting a description of Lakota Catholic grieving rituals raises the awareness that they are part of an already merged culture. Terms used to describe the integration between the Christian tradition and the cultures of the world are "adaptation," "accommodation," "indigenization" and "gospel in culture." Increasingly "contextualization" is becoming a preferred term in Christian theological circles. The Roman Catholic church has described Christianity's encounter with culture by using the word "inculturation."

Inculturation was a concept originally developed and used in the field of psychology. As now used in Roman Catholic theology, inculturation refers to the ongoing exchange between faith and culture. "Inculturation is the incarnation of the Gospel in the hereditary cultures, and at the same time, the introduction of these cultures into the life of the Church." (John Paul II, 1985) At times the Roman Catholic church has spoken in terms of "translating" the faith into the culture, but that relationship is too one directional. Inculturation means that Christianity is also open to being transformed and enhanced by its encounter with a culture.

Native Americans have always borrowed customs that prove spiritually enhancing. (McGaa, p.45) But to what degree has inculturation taken place? As Christian and Lakota traditions of grieving were first introduced to one another, they were practiced side by side with little religious interpenetration. Today there is more of an attempt being made at the integration which is necessary for a true inculturation. (Black Bear Jr.)

Paul Steinmetz S.J. describes an approach to religion shared by many Lakota Catholics:

> Some Lakota easily pass from the traditional to the Christian religious system, and vice versa according to

13

the spiritual needs of the moment. Because their traditional religion offers limited information on the final
destiny of souls, they welcome the resurrection of Christ
as a guarantee of eternal life. (Peelman, p. 139)

Peelman (p. 77) uses the word "dimorphism" to categorize the
encounter between Lakota religion and Christianity. Some integration
and change have taken place, but the traditional world view of Lakota
people has been retained. Stolzman, (p. 209) who is sometimes criti-
cized for paralleling Lakota and Christian religions too neatly, describes
the two religions as fitting together like a hand and glove, touching in
many places. The two share much in common but remain separate.
Robert Schreiter offers a category of Dual Theologies to describe a
merging where:

> The local culture accepts the sign system of the
> invading culture, but believes that there are still problems
> that the invading culture's sign system does not adequately
> handle. For those problems and issues, segments of the
> old system are maintained. (Schreiter p. 156)

Doris Hump explains what being Lakota and Christian means to her:

> **Some people that have strong Indian Religion
> want to stay away from church. They said God gave
> the Indians that pipe and God gave the whites the
> bible to pray with. I don't think white; I don't think
> Lakota. I always ask God to give me the under-
> standing that I don't want to do the wrong thing.**
> (*Doris Hump*)

When people do not dichotomize religious belief into the categories of
white or Lakota, an integration is beginning to take place. **"The majority
of the people do whatever feels comfortable to them. They come to
both Christian and Indian [traditions] to do grief work."** (*Rev. Richard
Charging Eagle*)

The US Catholic Bishops, writing a pastoral letter on American
Indians, urged "The Gospel message must take root and grow within
each culture and each community." (USCC 1977 #8) They call for the

national and diocesan liturgical offices to help Indian communities incorporate not only their language, but their native prayer forms into liturgy and other worship services. (USCC 1977, #26)

The Roman Catholic church sees the gospel as transcending cultures and acting as an agent which purifies and adds to cultures. It also acknowledges the need to borrow elements of cultures to make the gospel message known. (*Evangelii Nuntiandi*, #20, in Flannery) The church is catholic, that is, universal, through the act of embracing people of varying races, languages and cultures. The Second Vatican Council's document, *Gaudium et Spes* (# 53, in Flannery), teaches that the human person can achieve true and full humanity only by means of culture.

Distinct cultures are a rich heritage of each human community. The church calls itself to "do everything possible to make all persons aware of their right to culture and their duty to develop themselves culturally." (GS # 60) "The easy human decision that reckons unity as uniformity and oneness as the enemy of pluralism, must be denied." (USCC 1980, p. 2)

The SEDOS research seminar called the Roman Catholic church to be a real and significant protector of ancestral religions and of the values of God's reign found in them. Sometimes the more powerful of the dialogue partners must absorb pain and become a suffering servant, in defense of the other tradition. (SEDOS)

But inculturation does not happen without tension. As the gospel increasingly takes root in local cultures the urgent question becomes how to measure what is genuinely Christian and what is not. The other hotly debated question is who judges what is a valid integration of Christianity and the culture.

Roman Catholic theology is very systematic. While the goal of inculturation expressly desires liturgical innovations, those always must be cleared through the conference of bishops, "to weigh carefully and prudently what elements from the traditions and culture of individual peoples may be appropriately admitted into divine worship, then to propose to the Apostolic See adaptations considered useful or necessary." (ICEL, 1982, #38)

Lakota theology, on the other hand, is a wisdom type of theology.

15

Unlike systematic theology it is a way of living in the world, rather than a sure knowledge style of theology. (Schreiter p. 43) "It is not a matter of doctrine but of life experienced in the immediate context of extended family, clan, tribe, people and nation." (Peelman, p. 17) Like many cultures, the Lakota had no word for "religion" because it was not something separable from life. In looking at religious actions and the reasons behind them, not everything is explainable. Even *Wakan Tanka*, the phrase usually used of God, is often translated as "Great Mystery." Lakota spirituality leaves room for mystery and the unknown. It values personal experience, dreams and visions. (Peelman, p. 41) Each person is encouraged to seek and follow one's own vision, including the vision and practice of Lakota traditional ways. The ability to accept multiple religious truths can clash with a Roman Catholic theology which strives for a well developed body of doctrine and precise definitions.

The description of Lakota ritual presented in this chapter is not a set of duties to be followed exactly, with proper rubrics and words. The Lakota tradition is a resource that people will draw upon as it helps them navigate their way through their grieving. People will make adaptations that are practical. They will use what helps them and makes sense to them. A range of grieving activities therefore exists, depending upon a family's own appropriation of those traditions.

> In all societies . . . the issue of death throws into
> relief the most important cultural values by which people
> live their lives and evaluate their experiences. Life
> becomes transparent against the background of death,
> and fundamental social and cultural issues are revealed.
> (Huntington and Metcalf, p. 2)

This study highlights the cultural values which are revealed and reinforced through Lakota Catholic grieving practices. The practices provide a model to teach the community how to grieve and what it means to be Lakota. The practices also express beliefs about God's action and the community's response to the deaths in its midst. Before examining Lakota Catholic grieving practices as they exist now, it might be helpful to explore early Lakota practice before any merging with Christian ways

16

began.

EARLY LAKOTA PRACTICES:

Before Western contact on the Great Plains the Lakota funerary practice was to wrap the bodies of their dead in blankets or robes and place them on scaffolding. The burial took place on the fourth day after death, which is the period of time that the spirit would wander the earth before saying farewell to the body. (Riggs p. 212) Public wakes were held with time for speeches, both to speak about the one who had died and to pass on spiritual teachings to those gathered. The deceased was left with what they might need on their journey to the spirit world. Personal property was bundled and placed with them, including their favorite dog, or later, their horse. They were dressed in fine clothes to be well dressed and prepared for the entrance into the spirit world. (Black Bear Jr., p. 4B) Animals and elements eventually returned the body to the earth from which it came. Later the bones were gathered up and buried in a mound. (Riggs, p. 212)

> People placed the dead bodies where savage animals could not disturb them and beside the bodies food and all that they possessed . . . the spirit-like self of things abandoned in the name of the dead became the spiritual possessions of the departing spirit and were taken on the spirit trail to the spirit world where they were enjoyed forever. Kindred and friends added to the possessions of the dead gifts according to their ability, often impoverishing themselves . . . that all they gave in this way would be found in the spirit world to enrich the givers when they came there. (Walker, 1983, p. 374)

The family underwent a ritual grieving process that traditionally lasted a year. If a mother died, the man would take a new wife to provide for the children. If a father died, his wife would be taken into the camp of her husband's brother, or a member of the extended family, *tiyospaye*. An older widow could move back with her brothers. People were always provided for. The grieving process also solidified other relationships within the *tiyospaye*. This was best exemplified when a child died,

17

through a rite called "Ghost-owning."

> For a year the bereaved parents faithfully preserved a lock of their dead child's hair to show their respect. . . . In this interim they underwent rigidly prescribed attendance rites, and also devoted their time, often with the help of relatives, to the accumulation of great stores of clothing, utensils, horses, and even food. At the expiration of the time, amid the final ceremony and feasting, the parents gave to the people assembled everything they had collected throughout the year . . . giving till it hurt . . . when everything was distributed the couple would dismantle their tipi and offer it to someone, an act which was followed by the final gesture of removing their clothes and giving them away. Alone, in their nakedness, with neither possession nor dwelling nor food, a man and wife thus displayed before all the Sioux's highest ideal of generosity combined with the utmost tribute for one beloved. (Hassrick, p. 38)

Shortly after such a ceremony, others would begin to repay the generosity by taking care of the couple, feeding, and clothing them. The exchange of goods also helped establish communal relationships.

Giving away all the property of the deceased was the norm and the tradition has carried on in various forms to this day. A contemporary Lakota, Severt Young Bear explains,

> When you have material possessions, the best thing you can do with them is to give them away, especially to those who are without or are having a hard time. A leader is not the guy who can store up and keep lots of things, but instead someone who will share them with the people. We are taught as young boys and girls that in order to honor ourselves and our relatives, we should always be ready to share . . . It's funny, when you think of the Christian principle of charity, that once we were put on reservations, both the missionaries and the BIA

18

opposed the sharing of material goods because it kept us from becoming modern, self-supporting American citizens. (Young Bear, pp. 57 - 58)

Ironically giveaways were objected to not on the grounds they were contrary to the gospel, but that they were contrary to the Protestant work ethic! Lakota persons gained status not by how much they saved, but by how generously they gave of their possessions. The government succeeded in outlawing giveaways for a time and also outlawed the use of funeral scaffolding. All bodies thus had to be buried in the ground. This practice of burial for Lakota people is only about a century old. The coffin has changed over the years from a blanket to wrap the body, to a do-it-yourself coffin made with precut lumber purchased at the local hardware store, to modern metal coffins and vaults. J.D. Kessling has been doing the undertaking work on Cheyenne River Reservation for more than 60 years, beginning in 1934. During those days tribal members only needed him to do the embalming that the state required. They handled everything else on their own. Kessling explained that the major shift toward purchasing caskets and other funeral home services began during World War II when Lakota soldiers killed in the war were sent home and the government paid for the caskets and funerals which included full military honors.

CURRENT PRACTICES

From the time they are born, Lakota people learn about death and grief through participation in all the functions of the Lakota community. Members of the community learn through observation of rituals and verbal instruction by elders. Because people attend wakes and funerals from early childhood onward, they observe how they are expected to behave. It is understood that by virtue of attending, one will know all one needs to know. (Brokenleg and Middleton, p. 105)

Observing what is done, and listening to what is said, particularly by the elders, are keys to learning about Lakota culture. Participating in funerals and wakes in that way brought me to some initial understandings

19

of what one needs to know. Those insights were deepened by parish-ioners who willingly shared about their beliefs and rituals.

VIGIL AT THE TIME OF DEATH

When a person is dying, the extended family gathers to be with them.

In Indian, the grieving part begins from the time the person gets sick until the time they die. To us, the Lakota, we take that as a very sacred time. A very *wakan* time. From the time somebody's getting sick, and you know that the person is not going to recover, people start going to these people's homes. Families are going to start praying, and talking to them and preparing them for that death. (*Rev. Richard Charging Eagle*)

In the Lakota way, your mother's sisters are also your mother. Your father's brothers are also your father. Given the importance of family, no Lakota person wants to die alone. Generally large families make for many mourners. While the off-reservation hospitals normally restrict the number of visitors that can be in the room at any one time, the Indian Health Services staff of the local Public Health Hospital does not enforce such a set of rules. Cheyenne River Reservation has no nursing home and the hospital is small with no surgical facilities. Often the hospital is more like a hospice, where people are sent home to die when there is no more that can be done for them at the distant regional hospitals. In the room of a terminally ill patient, ten or fifteen family members might be crowded around the bed. If the family group is larger than that, and it almost always swells when death is near, people may also be assembled in the hallway.

When the dying person is not suffering from a long term illness, but from trauma, like an accident or a sudden heart attack, it is again the hospital which receives them. Word gets out quickly, mostly through the reservation's word-of-mouth informal network, when people are taken to the emergency room. Families quickly stream there to wait for news of loved ones.

The Lakota tradition has prayer songs for, and sometimes by, the dying. Bravery is one of the cardinal Lakota virtues. Especially in the warrior societies, people were encouraged to face death bravely. A song attributed to Crazy Horse calls and proclaims, "**Hoka hey!** Follow me; Today is a good day to fight; Today is a good day to die." Lakota people are expected to face their own deaths bravely. The Lakota teach that no one knows when they will be asked to surrender to death, so fearless living is the proper response until that time comes.

> **I work with elderly people. Their grieving seems not to be like the younger people. You don't find many elderly people that fear death. We always talk about the wisdom keepers. They've lived through their sons dying and whatever. You don't learn that anywhere, you just live it.** (*Iyonne Garreau*)

Tears of mourning are for others more than for oneself. Another example of a Mourning Song is this lament, chanted by an elderly person who is having a difficult time and may be close to dying.

> I am going to lie somewhere, so I stand. I say this and stand with courage. (Black Bear, p. 125)

For Roman Catholics the sacrament of Anointing of the Sick is also seen as a way to give strength and courage. The Catholic pastoral staff's practice has been to encourage that Anointing of the Sick be celebrated as soon as someone becomes seriously ill, rather than waiting for the dying moment. People ask for this sacrament regularly and anointings are frequently celebrated in church or at home, with the presence of as many family members as possible to add their prayers and support.

Sage is used by the Lakota to repel and drive away any evil spirits. The room is purified by burning sage, often with an accompanying song. The smoke is spread throughout the room, using an Eagle Feather if one is available, as people wave the smoke over themselves in a ritual washing. *Azilya* is the Lakota term for this act of incensing. This is also referred to as "smudging." If a pipe carrier[1] is present, the pipe is passed around for each to smoke, or touched to the lips of the dying person if they are unable to smoke the pipe on their own. **Cannunpa yuha**

21

wocekiye is the term for the Pipe Ceremony.

When prayers and rituals are finished, the family waits for death with the dying person. There may be a sharing of traditional Lakota foods. The time often contains tears, talking to the dying person and to one another. Often there is silence. Ministers often wait in silent vigil with the family, available if people feel the need or desire to talk.

When death occurs, parishioners ask their spiritual leaders to offer prayers. Prayers of most any kind are appreciated and encouraged. I usually began with some formal ritual, using the prayers for the dead from the Roman Ritual of Pastoral Care of the Sick. I blessed the body by sprinkling holy water and prayed a short form of the Litany of the Saints. That was more familiar to older Lakota Catholics than younger ones. After death, people have a tendency to feel numb and shocked. A repeated ritual response like "pray for us" invites people into participation and moves them out of inactivity. The participation can start to make the reality of a loss sink in, while not requiring spontaneity or processing that the grievers may not be ready for.

After the ritual prayers comes a movement into more personal prayer, or words that needed to be spoken. One way that often facilitated this movement was to join mourners in a circle of support, holding hands and praying the Lord's Prayer together. I would offer a spontaneous, personal prayer for the one who had died and for health and healing in the family. Health and healing are important gifts to be prayed for in Lakota spirituality. Then any family member who had words or prayers were invited to speak.

Most often one of the family elders will speak to the other mourners. Depending on the speaker, words might be in Lakota, English, or some combination. They identify some of what the family is feeling. If a mother or father has died, they might comment about how hard it is to be an orphan. The death of a child might bring prayers for the parents in their

[1]The sacred pipe, known as **Ptehincala hu cannunpa**, the White Buffalo Calf Pipe, is central to Lakota religious belief and ritual. The pipe has great power, and is a mediator between the Lakota nation and God In a pipe ceremony, the pipe is offered to the spirits of each of the four directions, as well as to grandmother earth, and the grandfather above, as their help is invoked. The Lakota consider the pipe a living entity given to them so the people might live. Pipe carriers are those who use a pipe of their own for prayer These pipes are blessed from, and draw their power from the White Buffalo Calf Pipe. For more explanation about the sacred pipe's significance, see Arval Looking Horse. (DeMallie and Parks, pp. 67-73)

22

time of loss. Family members are exhorted to lean on each other for the strength to carry on. The heart felt words make a lasting impression.

The nearest funeral home is 90 miles away, so there is no quick removal of the body, but a lengthy wait until the undertaker comes. Usually the family stays with the body and with one another, doing some leave taking. Before the body is removed, each of the relatives who choose to may go into the room one last time. Often grieving people talk out loud, often directing their words to the spirit of the one who has died. On some occasions I observed the family work with a nurse to wash and clean up the body. There is generally little fear about touching the dead body, as people hug, or hold the hand of the dead. The young men in the family, especially the sons and grandsons, may aid the undertaker when he arrives. Sometimes the dead are escorted to the hearse with as much dignity as they will have in the funeral procession. Traditional Lakota people may wrap the body in a blanket and place sage in their hands.

Historically, warriors painted their faces before battle so God could see their faces clearly if they had to die. Some people still have their faces painted after death occurs:

> **They paint people's faces if they Sun Dance[2], or if they're a medicine man, or go through a *hunkayapi*** (making of relatives) **ceremony - the people that at one time in their life went through a ceremony and had their faces painted. When they die, they have their face painted, because that's the way the spirits see them at that ceremony, so they'll recognize them when they go into the spirit world.** *(Darlene Young Bear)*

PREPARATION FOR FUNERAL

Getting ready for a funeral normally takes many days. The ideal number of days between death and burial, in the Lakota way, is four. While people strive to stay within that limit, as much as a week may be

[2]The Sun Dance is the most important ritual of traditional Lakota religion. Black Elk (J. E. Brown pp. 67-100) and Amiotte (DeMallie and Parks pp. 75-89) provide good introductions. See Holler (1995) for a more detailed description and historical overview.

given if relatives who live at a distance need to make the journey home. This time is where the *tiyospaye*, the extended family, pulls together.

> **I remember when we were young. People would come and they would camp for days. It was [a time of] reaffirming relationships, getting to know your other relatives. It was like a big get-together, for those three or four days.** (*Rosie Roach Avery*)

Interconnections are reaffirmed and relationships indeed strengthened as the family begins baking and cooking for the meals and making and/or purchasing items to be used if an honoring giveaway will take place. Women handle most of the cooking, though men are generally in charge of the butchering and large scale stew and soup making. It is also the men's role to dig the grave if the family does not get someone with a backhoe to take care of it. Children will help as they are able.

> **Families also want to keep even the young ones busy during that time. They might be helping in the kitchen or with the cleaning, watching the little ones. They are always included, always have something to do during that time.** (*Rosie Roach Avery*)

The Families who practice the tradition of the *inipi*, or sweat bath, may use that ceremony to purify and strengthen themselves by prayer.[3]

If someone you are related to dies, you are expected to drop everything and go and attend to the family.

> **When we were growing up, they would take the whole family and they'd go and stay with them all the way through. Today we call and see if there's anything we can do to support them in what they're going through. There's so many things like feeding people, so many people to call. Sometimes you're probably going through the night.** (*Rosie Roach Avery*)

---

[3]The *inipi* is a communal prayer ritual held in a small dome shaped lodge, made of a wooden frame and covered with canvas or hides. Participants sit around a pit filled with red hot rocks. During the prayer water is poured over the rocks to produce a steam that purifies. Prayers are offered and the spirits' help is invoked. The ritual lasts through four rounds of steam and prayer. See Black Elk (Brown, pp. 31-43) for a description.

Lakota tradition calls for the burning of the dead person's clothes. One individual may do the burning, or the entire family may gather together for a ritual that can evoke so many memories of what is being lost. Family members may ask for some object, like a picture, as a keepsake, but generally, every personal possession, especially clothes or anything that was soiled by the person is burnt up.

Meanwhile, in the evenings, prayers are offered in the family home. Neighbors and relatives stop by, bringing food, money and items to be used for the giveaway. They offer words of sympathy and ask about times and plans for the services. This is one of many times that friends, relatives and neighbors will reach out a sympathetic and helping hand to those who are grieving. They are received with gratitude and respect.

When my mother passed away, I remember people coming to the house and they'd go around and shake our hands. My dad, told me, "When somebody comes to shake your hand, you stand up." When he passed away, I always remember you did that. When we were sitting in the pews, people would go up there and whenever they come up and shake our hands I always stood up. (*Marty Ward*)

The gift of food and the chance to visit can be quite touching. One woman put it, "Our family brings this food to share with you to give you some strength, which you need in your time of sadness." The visitors often recount how difficult life was for them when a loved one died and they offer their prayers and support.

In helping people remember the one who has died, some families may put together pictures of, or memorabilia from, the dead, making a display in the home. This practice seems to help people focus on their relationship with the one who has died and triggers memories which lead to story telling. Such rituals can remind people of the reality of the death and prompt feelings and acknowledgment of the loss.

Ministers are also expected to drop by the home to visit and pray. In the small reservation communities, deaths cross all religious boundaries. When a Roman Catholic dies and the relatives come together, it is inevitable that some of the *tiyospaye* belong to other traditions. The Episcopal and Congregational churches are the largest of several Christian churches on the reservation. Some family members exclusively practice traditional Lakota Religion. Yet an ecumenical spirit predominates, as people from all these traditions gather to pray and to support the family.

Even in the homes, some ministers devote the better part of their visit and prayer preaching to the family. The Catholic Pastoral Team found it helpful to develop home prayer services that actively involve those who gather, with hymn singing, common prayer with the psalms, and the invitation for spontaneous intercessory prayer.

The family shows hospitality to all who come by serving some of the soup, cake and sandwiches that have been dropped off at the house. Sharing food is an important part of every Lakota gathering. On the Western end of the reservation, where the Lakota language and traditions are strongest, prayer services in the home before a funeral are more common than in the other communities.

Even if there is no home prayer service, it is appropriate for the pastoral team member leading funeral services to visit the home as soon as possible to discuss arrangements with the family. Because individuals have vastly different appropriations of the Lakota and Christian traditions, no two funerals ever followed the same pattern.

> **On the reservation here, most of the families are Indian and some of the families might be considered "the traditional" with the wake and the funeral and then a year later having a ceremony. But some families don't do that either. Some families might just want a rosary or a small chapel service the night before the funeral. If you're going to practice in a cultural area, whether it be Native American or whatever, you need to realize, not all Indians are traditional Indians.** *(Eileen Peacock)*

Decisions about honor songs, *azilya*, who will be asked or expected to speak, and pipe ceremonies, all depend on the practices of the partic-

26

ular family. Lakota rituals are practiced with an internal consistency by the individual, but in infinite variety from person to person. How to pray is often related to a personal vision. While some parishioners come to an integration of Lakota traditions and Catholicism, the religious practices of people that ask Roman Catholic ministers to lead the services range from those who are exclusively Catholic to those engaged in only Lakota traditions. It can also include those who practice neither tradition. In planning with the family, ministers can go over options and find ways that help the family ritualize both their faith and their grieving.

After planning is done, people stay around the house talking, preparing, passing time. The family may recollect stories about the person, and how the death is affecting them. A question like, "What will you remember most about (name)?" can often focus the family on a meaningful discussion. Even the children can add their memories and perceptions. The stories can elicit tears, laughter, pain and many other intense emotions. Getting people to talk about the dead, rather than staying in denial, helps along the grieving process. This is facilitated even more by the Lakota value of being with one another during times of grieving. Listening to stories about the dead person's life can also help the one preaching to get a sense of what they were about and what questions the death has raised about people's faith and understanding of the meaning of life.

While I emphasize the positive aspects of these rituals, the reality is more complex. Within the *tiyospaye,* alcohol and strained relationships can complicate the grieving enormously. The extended family system is often under severe stress at these times and dysfunction surfaces. Some people try to numb the pain by drinking, which adds more stress on everyone else. But generally, people pull together and help one another through.

Ecumenical cooperation is often complicated by theological approaches that seemingly contradict one another. One minister might focus on God's love and the next use language that triggers guilt feelings. Still, churches have great potential for ecumenism on the reservation, because the people are more concerned with how to live in the world and do not worry much about doctrinal disagreements.

WAKES

There are no funeral homes on the reservation, so no tradition of waking people in a funeral chapel has been established. Wakes are generally held in churches. Some communities have community/cultural centers which can also be used for wakes. If the funeral is very large, especially if it is for a child in the school system, the school gymnasium or auditorium may be used. The separation between church and state is less of an issue on the reservation. A Lakota worldview questions why western culture tries to dichotomize civil and religious practice anyway. Both are part of life. A few people choose to hold the wake in their homes, though this practice is becoming less common.

Traditionally, wakes last all night. No individual is expected to stay up all night, though some may choose to. Family members shuttle home to sleep, shower, or change clothes. Visitors are free to come and go as they need to, but some member of the family will keep the vigil with their loved one throughout the night, until the time of the funeral.

An elderly Lakota woman recounted the first time she went to a "white" funeral. After the rosary, the altar society served cake and coffee. Just as she was settling into the conversation, people started leaving and sons and daughter of the woman being waked started gathering their belongings to leave. "I could not believe they were going to leave their mother alone by herself in the church all night! Didn't they know how lonely she would feel and how much she needed them around to help her through this hard time of death?" Her relationship with the spirit of her dead friend was still very real and tangible for her.

Many Roman Catholic wakes begin with the traditional rosary. A parish minister might start the prayer, then invite members of the assembly to take a turn leading one of the decades. For the immediate family that will probably be too much to ask emotionally, but for friends, cousins, aunts or uncles, it encourages participation and lay leadership of prayer. For families unfamiliar with that prayer form, a prepared scripture service that members of the assembly can follow along and respond to is often used. The pastoral team developed a series of booklets for people to use that incorporate adaptations of psalms and prayers which reflect a Native American perspective.

As is true with the home prayer services, wakes are as ecumenical as the family is. After the rosary or scriptural service, other ministers present are invited to speak, pray, or share some words from scripture. Roman Catholic ministers are likewise invited to participate in services at other churches. Throughout the night, anyone who wants to speak or pray can, which again shows an openness to multiple religious traditions. Musicians drop in and offer songs, either traditional Lakota honor songs, or more often, a brand of country gospel songs. They usually share some words of witness.

When listening to different preachers present a multitude of conflicting theologies at wakes, I often wondered how people integrated all they were hearing. In asking parishioners about this, they were quite honest in saying that what they did not like they just tuned out. Lakota culture puts a high value on autonomy. Leaders, in both the political and religious spheres, really only have authority when people agree with the truth of their positions. The real work of the wake went on with the gathering, the sharing of the meal, renewing family ties and remembering. People use the time to talk and tell stories about the one who had died, as a way of beginning to memorialize them.

Cultural elements that may be found in Lakota wakes may include a ritual receiving of the body and blessing the area with sage. *Tom Eagle Staff* explained the Lakota traditionally honor fallen warriors and Sun Dancers by placing a pipe filled with tobacco, and kept intact until the burial, near the body. A buffalo skull, which is a medium for prayers and a buffalo robe, which represents an altar, are also placed near the body. When the body is moved, the pipe is carried by a young woman, who represents the White Buffalo Calf Woman, who gave the Lakota the sacred pipe. Because of the respect Lakota hold for the pipe, if a pipe is present, it should lead any procession.

After formal services are completed, people drift between church and hall, where coffee and cake are always at hand. Often meals are served as well. Traditionally, meals began at midnight, but increasingly, immediately following services. A plate of food is set aside for the spirit of the deceased. When the wake is in the cultural center or community building, people eat in the same space they pray in. Even in view of the body, conversations freely flow.

In addition to food, tobacco is prevalent at wakes and funerals. Tobacco is sacred, *wakan*, for the Lakota. Piles of loose cigarettes are heaped onto serving dishes and placed on tables throughout the hall. Even people who never smoke elsewhere will light up a cigarette at a wake.

If the person who dies has served in the armed forces, one of the veterans groups lead ritual of their own. Military honors have always been deemed special in the traditionally warrior-based Lakota society. Colors, and sometimes an honor guard, are posted. At a candlelight roll call,

> **They turned off all the lights and lit a candle above dad. All you could see was him. Somebody called out the names of all the veterans who were at the church and they answered, 'Here sir!' Then they called dad's name and no one answered. I got a big lump in my throat. I was wanting to answer for him. We were waiting for him to walk through the doors and say 'Here Sir!' Then somebody else answered, 'He is not here sir! He has gone on to a higher command!' That was pretty touching there.** (*Tater and Marty Ward*)

Afterwards, each veteran in the assembly approaches the casket, salutes, then goes to the family, shakes hands and offers their sympathy. Throughout the entire time of ritual grieving, well wishers repeatedly approach the family and offer words of sympathy and a hand shake. This can evoke a strong emotional response. While that may be difficult for the family, it also brings home the reality of the loss, while offering them support.

No one is expected to interact with people all of the time. Especially when the wakes are held in churches which have a separate hall, as the focus of activity shifts to the meal and conversation, people who need to be alone will work their way back into the church and spend time with their own thoughts, or leave and go home to come back later. The benefit of these gatherings is that wakes promote interaction for people in grief. Stories are told and relationships renewed. Tears mingle with memories and laughter. The expression of feelings and the making of memories promote healthy initial grieving.

FUNERAL MASS

Funerals are normally scheduled for weekday mornings, around ten or eleven o'clock. While in many places funerals have increasingly become the function of the immediate family, on Cheyenne River Reservation friends and neighbors take time off their jobs and children stay home from school. People who ranch or farm rearrange their chores to attend funerals. Tribal workers have a generous leave policy that allows them to attend most funerals. In an area with high unemployment, that negative factor also contributes to the pool of people who can come.

While there is an announced time for beginning the funeral, the starting time depends on other factors. If the funeral director has another funeral to attend to, or a veteran is scheduled for burial in the Black Hills National Cemetery at a set time, there is more pressure to start as close to on time as possible. But mostly people filter in and the family decides when everyone who needs to be there has arrived. When a key family member is delayed this can mean a wait of several hours.

In Lakota ritual the focus is not on clock time, the focus is on the activity itself. It is better to think of Lakota ritual time in terms of order — doing things according to priorities. A ceremony takes precedence over all other activities. People sacrifice other activities in order to be present for the ceremony. They place themselves in a proper frame of mind and the ceremony takes as long as it takes to do it correctly. Length of clock time, short or long, is irrelevant. (Hatcher, 1996)

31

While the family tries to plan who will be present to sing, offer an honor song, or say a few words about the deceased and about the grief the assembly is experiencing, that is subject to change depending who shows up and who does not. Up until the time the funeral begins (and even sometimes during) the presider acts as a master of ceremonies in trying to coordinate some order of who is up next. Flexibility is a helpful quality for organizers and presiders to possess.

Floral arrangements have become a normal part of Lakota funerals. Often they are shaped like horses, medicine wheels, or the family's livestock brand, to personalize the memorial.

Close to the beginning of the funeral mass, the funeral director announces that the casket will be closed for the last time and gives people the chance to pay their last respects. Depending on the group, this process can take several minutes, or even an hour. Rather than a brief filing past, each person takes the amount of time they need to pray and pay their respects. Open weeping is common. Some people address words to the deceased. Afterwards they approach the family and offer a handshake and their condolences. This evokes more outpouring of emotion. The immediate family is the last to take leave of the body.

Objects placed in the casket are usually personal reminders of the dead. Pictures are most common, as are cigarettes, a favorite hat, beadwork, or a pow-wow dress. Women who danced often have a shawl draped over an arm. There is no required way to dress the body, although many insist that the clothing be new, after all the old clothes have been burned. There is nothing necessarily distinguishing about the way mourners dress, although men with long hair will let it hang loosely rather than wearing it in a tail when they are grieving. Traditionally a woman would respond to her husband's death by cutting her hair and gouging herself with a knife. Today the gouging practice is rare. I never observed anyone who had ritually slashed themselves. The cutting of hair has remained a part of the tradition. Some may wrap their hair in a cloth and place it in the casket. Traditionally mourners painted their faces black and asked the spirits to pity those grieving. Walker points out that black was also a symbol of human passion grief, anger, or determination.

(Walker, 1982, p. 99)

At the end of the nineteenth century Short Bull explained to Walker,

> We blacken our faces and cause our blood to flow from wounds so that the Wakan Tanka will know that we sincerely mourn for our dead. We give to the departing spirits what they need on the trail and in the spirit world. If we enrich the spirits with our gifts, they will go into the spirit world with pride and honor and all we give will be there for us when our spirits come there. If we give nothing to the dead, then their spirits will come into the spirit world with only shame. (Walker, 1991, p. 142)

Black is no longer a dominant color during funerals. But many people still recognize its symbolism and significance.

Once the casket is closed, the Roman Catholic funeral rites call for the placing of the pall or other Christian symbols. More often, the pall bearers drape a star quilt over the casket. Star quilts are given to honor and to show respect. As was the case when the dead were wrapped in blankets and placed on the scaffold, the star quilt will go to the grave with the person being buried. Some still place the traditional red cloth over the coffin, as red is the most sacred of all Lakota colors.

If there is a procession with the casket into church, it usually involves many people. Besides the six to eight men designated as pall bearers, there is also a group of honorary pall bearers, sometimes as many as twenty. These include elderly persons for whom carrying the casket is physically challenging, and friends. Women are generally, though not always, honorary pall bearers. A pipe or drum may also lead the body. The family gathers around the casket at the back of church and, during the opening song, processes behind the pallbearers to their pews. In the case of the very small churches, which are usually filled to overflowing for funerals, logistics prevent processions. Instead, the casket is already in the front of the altar when people arrive.

The Liturgy of the Word and Liturgy of the Eucharist proceed much as they would most anywhere else in the U.S. with only a few unique features. *Azilya*, the ritual incensing, may be done at several points

33

during the liturgy. *Azilya* is appropriate during the penitential rite as a sign of purification, but funeral liturgies have no penitential rite. The Book of The Gospels may be honored by being blessed with sage before being proclaimed. During the Preparation of the Gifts, besides incensing the altar and gifts, it is the practice to bless the body and the assembly. In the planning, the families themselves can help determine if sage, sweet grass, or incense is most appropriate. Sage is more commonly used to purify and sweet grass to bless. Families might also suggest an *azilya* at other times, such as the beginning or the end of the services.

At some point during the mass an "honor song" is sung in Lakota, using the person's Indian name. The honor song is usually after communion, but also is sung at the beginning or end of the funeral. There are different versions, depending on the singer and their relationship to the deceased. Here is a sampling of a few of the honor songs:

> Friend, pause and look this way (3 times), Say ye,
>
> a grandson (granddaughter) of (name) is coming.
>
> (Riggs, p. 213)

There are different kinds of songs. They sing those songs when somebody dies. There's one: 'you will miss him, or you will not see him again.' This song is used when someone died. It's just a short song, but it's sung over and over again. "Where are you? Where are you going? Are you going over? Did you go? Where are you going? My relatives are crying for you." (*Elsie Slides Off*)

God, your son (or daughter) is coming home Going home to God He's (she's) coming home. He's (she's) coming home Us ordinary humans, we think human so love us. Have pity on us. (*Ted Knife*)

(his name), he is gone and I'm having a hard time.

I'm having a hard time.

But this earth goes a long ways. (*Darlene Young Bear*)

These Lakota honor songs sung at the time of death have much in common with the lamentation tradition found in Judeo-Christian scriptures. They allow for honest and heart felt expressions of the feelings of loss evoked by death. Some songs are composed especially for the occasion.

After communion, before preparing to journey to the cemetery, the family might ask someone to say a few words about the deceased, offer a eulogy, or read an obituary. Sometimes friends or family members pen a poem in their memory and read that as well.

BURIAL

Most of the people who attend the funeral will also make the journey to the cemetery for burial as well. A few of the churches have cemeteries adjacent, while some of the cemeteries are as far as forty miles from the church. The funeral director has some hearses that are four wheel drive suburbans, because getting to the remote locations requires crossing open prairie and creek beds. When the cemetery is close by, the casket is usually carried by the pall bearers from the church to the grave. One family carried their mother's body almost a half mile to the cemetery, led by a drum group singing honor songs. The rhythm of the pounding drum transformed the procession march into a sorrowful dance. For some of the Lakota ranchers, a horse and wagon may carry the dead. Mourners will carry the baskets of flowers from the church with them and use them to decorate the grave when the burial is complete.

Few of the cemeteries are neatly manicured with plush green grass. Most have native prairie grasses and even weeds. The huge pile of dirt unearthed to create the grave usually sits uncovered, an obstacle mourners have to navigate around. While a few people are now using vaults, most of the rough boxes are just that, made of plywood. In the stark simplicity, death always seemed very tangible.

Songs are common at the cemetery. They may be out of the Christian tradition like "Amazing Grace," or "The Old Rugged Cross," or may be an occasion for an honor song. The Lakota singers are almost exclusively men, though this practice is changing some. Women add trills for emphasis.

The Order of Christian Funerals calls for a blessing of the grave, a final commendation, and blessing the gathered mourners. In addition, there may be prayers offered to Wakan Tanka for the deceased and the mourners by one of the **Wocekiye Wicasa** (men of prayer). Some traditional Lakota people will mark the grave's corners with four choke cherry tree branches as a symbolic reminder of the earlier practice of placing the dead on a scaffold.

Because of their beauty when flowing from riders in motion, ribbons were decoratively used on some Lakota clothing. Casket bearers wear ribbons pinned to their shirts and in preparation for lowering the casket, they remove them and place them on top of the casket. Other family members lay flowers. Some families have symbolic bouquets containing one flower for each of the children and grandchildren, who place the flowers on the casket as they file by. The funeral director usually removes the crucifix and asks the priest to bless it, presents it to the family and says a few personal words to them. Some traditional Lakota families may choose to have the "Releasing of the Spirit" ceremony at this time. One of the **Wocekiye Wicasa** present will lead the family in prayer with the pipe.

Veterans play taps for their fallen comrades as the casket is lowered into the ground. Guns are fired onto the prairie in salute. The U.S. Flag is presented to the family along with appreciation for their member's service. At first outsiders find it odd that Lakota so readily accept such patriotic military practices. In a warrior society, it was bravery in battle that gained honor. In addition, when the government outlawed so many Lakota gatherings and rituals, it was only on days like the fourth of July they were allowed group celebrations. They appropriated patriotic symbols as a way of keeping their underlying culture alive.

Young Bear explains how warriors sang death songs as they prepared for battles in which they might give their lives in sacrifice for their people.

36

Warriors sprinkled themselves with fine dust from a molehill and sang, recognizing that, like fine dust, their life would be gone soon. From the Kit Fox warrior society comes this example of one such song:

> I am a Kit Fox. I am supposed to die.
> If there is anything difficult, if there is anything dangerous
> That is mine to do. (Walker 1991, p. 270)

When a family heard of a death, they faced west and sang a death song, as opposed to facing east when they sing for a new baby. *Ic'ilowan,* the death song, is offered for the child they gave up that day. The mourning song is called **wicat olowan**. This is sung at the time of burial and again at the memorial service to end the year of mourning. (Young Bear, p. 84)

Rather than dispersing, the crowd stays until the coffin is completely buried.

> **By waiting until they bury the casket, I think that helps bring a sense of closure. It's final. The funerary rituals of the Lakota help give people the opportunity to get it [their emotions] out. I think that's the intent of the funerals. To get people to cry, to get it out of their system, to elicit a response from people.** (*Austin Keith*)

Several moments usually trigger upsurges of intense grief. When the coffin is lowered into the ground, when the undertaker nails the plywood top on the rough box, and when the first chunks of earth start to hit the wood, mourners squarely meet the reality of death. It is not shameful for anyone, including men, to cry during this time.

As the assembly begins to take its leave and prepare for a meal, it is customary to again approach each of the family members and shake hands, either in silence or by offering a few words. The men of the family bring shovels and pass them from hand to hand, taking turns filling in the grave themselves.

Since eagles fly highest of all the winged creatures, they are considered messengers of **Wakan Tanka** and signs of favor and blessing. People watch for them and when they are seen soaring above, it is a good sign for the one who has died and a comfort to the family.

FEED AND GIVEAWAY (*Wihpeyapi*)

As Little Wound put it, spirits are pleased with those who are generous and hate those who are stingy. (Walker, 1991, p. 67) Generosity is a central value for Lakota people, especially embodied during the post-burial feed and giveaway.

Everyone returns to the hall for a feed. A typical menu includes beef soup, sandwiches, potato salad, apples, fry bread, *wasna* made with meat, tallow and berries, and *wojapi*, a syrup-like fruit pudding made from berries and starch. A plate of food is prepared to nourish the spirits of the dead who are present. Decorated cakes are brought by friends sometimes with quite intricate frosted artwork, with "In memory of (name)" written on top. Often someone will walk around the hall displaying them for all to see before they are cut up and distributed. A few parishes have altar societies to coordinate the food, which is brought in by friends and relatives. In the smaller, more traditional Lakota communities, the *tiyospaye*, especially cousins and aunts, usually take on that task.

There is a social ordering in who gets served first, but it varies according to the situation. If a young child dies, the family may announce that they will feed the children first. If an aged person dies, then the elderly are often first in line. Sometimes the ministers and pall bearers are seated and a heaping plate of food is brought to them. There are no leftovers. All the food is passed out for people to take home and feed others (*wateca*). Sometimes these are staples for the very poor. Honor comes to those who can provide for those who have little.

I grew up with the expectations that if food was put in front of me, I had to clean my plate. At one of the first wakes I attended, the food kept coming and coming, so I ate and ate until my stomach ached. I still get kidded about that as an example of the outsider trying too hard to be culturally sensitive, without really understanding the culture. I later found out that it was OK to take a pass on seconds, or that I could have just placed a napkin over what remained on my plate and taken it home *wateca* style.

Historically, all the possessions of the dead were given away after their death. *Rev. Richard Charging Eagle* explains, "**Whatever they treasure**

38

the most, if you're hanging on to their spirit, they won't go home." Wealth was redistributed throughout society and the poor were taken care of. Brokenleg and Middleton believe the giving away of possessions helps the family begin a new and different life, without the physical reminders of the person. (Brokenleg and Middleton, p. 110) The *tiyospaye* would spend the next year making gifts and then give these away in honor of their departed relative the next year. *Peggy Knife* (page 70) explains that working toward the giveaway gave her a focus during a time that was emotionally difficult to deal with.

Today a giveaway may occur the day of the funeral, or may wait until the memorial, one year later, depending on the family's preference. Giveaways have become more a practice of honoring friends and relatives who helped the family in their time of grieving than a redistribution of social wealth. The giveaway shows that the person means more to you than any possession, so people give their best, with great generosity. *Darlene Young Bear* warns about preparing for a giveaway and not following through on your commitment:

> **If you're gonna do things like that and you set a
> date, you cannot postpone it. If you postpone it, to
> another date, things will not work out and you'll have
> to postpone it again. You really have to get every-
> thing done. Because like my grandparents said that
> spirit might come back. So go through with it. After
> you postpone it that spirit's gonna pout and make
> sure you have a hard time doing this again!** (*Darlene
> Young Bear*)

Besides special items belonging to the deceased, many new items are given away. Many families still make their own quilts and do beadwork, while others buy most of the items to be given away. Star quilts are a special honor to receive. The person whose name was called by the Master of Ceremonies comes forward and has the quilt draped around them. One who receives such a gift should thank and shake the hand of the family. Dance shawls and Pendleton blankets are also cherished gifts.

After individuals are honored, everyone in the assembly is given something, such as cigarettes, dish towels, candy bars, household goods, candy, sweet grass and handkerchiefs. These are offered in thanksgiving for their prayers for the dead. Most of the items are practical objects that people need in daily life.

Giveaways are extremely important to the Lakota. They are an expression of love and respect for the deceased. The giveaway also strengthens social ties with those who will offer support and help throughout the difficult time of loss.

KEEPING OF THE SOUL

Though not as common today as in the past, Lakota have a tradition of Keeping of the Soul for a one year period.

A lock of hair is cut from the head of the deceased, put into a special container, and put into a special place. One person is responsible every day for praying for, talking to, feeding, and protecting the soul from argument and spiritual contamination for one year. The guardian is to avoid drinking, arguing, fighting, and bad thoughts while performing sacrifices and gathering things so that in a year the soul may be spiritually well-prepared for its spirit journey. At the end of a year, the soul is ceremonially released with a feast, speeches, prayers and a request that the departed soul look back occasionally upon the loving relatives. (Stolzman p. 92)

When the soul bundle leaves the lodge or house, the soul is considered to be released to begin its final journey to the spirit world. Ben Black Bear, Jr. adds that since hair continues to grow even after death, the Lakota believe that the spirit of the individual is contained in the hair, and leaves the body through the hair.

In traditional olden times, they took the strand of hair wrapped in a red cloth. They put it inside the tipi and the tipi would be left all alone. Outside the tipi would be placed a plate right by the entrance way.

Every day a relative would make sure that plate had food in it. Anybody in the tribe who was hungry could come and eat, and they did that for a whole year. In addition to putting this plate of food out, they also had to practice patience, to try not to have ill feelings toward anybody for that whole year, be kind. That was the whole idea of keeping the soul, to have as much pleasantness surrounding it as possible.

Essentially it's a way of feeling like you have this person around with you still, for an additional year to provide some comfort. It was usually performed by a special member of the family that people were really attached to and couldn't quite let go of. It was a way of keeping this person, their soul, around for another year. After a year they had a releasing of the soul ceremony up near his gravesite where they took the hair out of the bundle and they burnt it in a fire. This was all preceded by a sweat lodge ceremony and different kinds of prayers. (*Austin Keith*)

Even if this ritual practice is not followed, the family will normally have a prayer service or mass of some kind, and a memorial feast a year after the death. They again thank friends who have helped them through their loss. Lakota people enter the grieving process with the expectation that grieving will take a significant amount of time. The effects on the family will last at least a year and longer. Commemorating the event one year later seems healthy. Grief cannot be passed over too quickly. It takes time to mourn.

WIPING OF TEARS

The wiping of tears ceremony may occur at the end of four days of grieving, or it may be held during the year anniversary memorial services. It is sometimes called "the giving of water and smoke" At a typical service,

> **A person came in and purified, with the burning of sweetgrass, for the family members, sang a song, prayed, gave them a drink of water and combed their hair. Usually if you're in grieving or mourning you usually stay away from the public and kind of keep to yourself. But this was a way that symbolized the need to go on with your life.** (*Rosie Roach Avery*)

The ritual also includes the use of tobacco, either in the smoking of a cigarette, or a *cannunpa*, sacred pipe. The person may be given something to eat as well.

> **The purpose of the water, is the water of life. The purpose of the tobacco is truth and sincerity. The food is like medicine. You've got to eat so you can live. Then they get the eldest of the community. A man and a woman (It could be a whole bunch), to talk to you now that you've come this far for four days. "Now we wipe your tears. We wipe your tears to come back to the community." They're part of the community again. We pray for them.** (*Rev. Richard Charging Eagle*)

The Lakota recognize that people need times to withdraw from activity and to be alone when grieving. The grieving practices are structured to allow that to happen. But they also call those grieving back into the circle of community.

> **They invite all the mourners to wipe their tears and they comb their hair and they give them water and they give them smoke and give them *wasna* meat. Each one that does that says to that person, "Come back into that circle. Come back to the circle now and be happy with us." If you don't cry and you don't have this ceremony done for you, it just makes things all the more hard on yourself.** (*Darlene Young Bear*)

While these rituals are celebrated with appropriate solemnity, there is also a playfulness and sense of humor that mark Lakota life in general. At the one year anniversary of one young girl's death, the master of ceremonies helped the family to re-enter into the life of the community by notifying the assembly that it was time to tell the "first joke." His corny anecdotes set a tone in which joking again became acceptable in relations with those who had stayed in the period of ritual grieving.

We can make fun of ourselves more than other people can. We just have a knack for that! People like my dad had a way of bringing humor into a real bad time. (*Iyonne Garreau*)

Belle had her leg amputated. Instead of the hospital getting rid of it, they asked us what we wanted to do with it. My grandfather and two grandchildren are buried at the top of a hill on our ranch. She said, "Take it upside the hill where the kids are buried. It will be all right up there. Literally speaking," she said, "that's what you call having one foot in the grave!" She joked about that. (*Louis Jewett*)

CEMETERY MEMORIALS

Throughout May, when the weather warms, each of the cemeteries has a set day when all those with relatives buried there gather for a memorial. These days are referred to as Decoration Days. Families are usually the only caretakers for the grave sites. In preparation for Decoration Day, people cut the grass, pull weeds, paint the wooden markers, replace rock edges that look uneven, and put "fresh" plastic flowers on the grave. A prayer service and blessing of the graves follow. Many of the graves are covered with food and gifts. A child's grave might be laden with packs of gum and cans of Coca-Cola. A grandmother's grave might contain Tupperware dishes and wash cloths. After the grave is blessed, a family member says something like, "We want to thank you for coming to honor and pray for our relative. We would like to share with you. All the children (or all the elderly women, men, etc.) can please take

43

something." Afterwards a meal is shared, picnic style, in and around the cemetery.

The dead are fed in remembrance at any meal, by setting aside a plate for them. Early mission writers note the placing of a kettle of hominy at the place the spirits were thought to be. (Hackman)

OTHER MEMORIALS

Individuals continually come up with ways to remember the dead that are meaningful to them. *Debbie Day's* son's classmates had a parade and float dedicated to him. In the rancher/cowboy tradition there are other ways to remember those who have died.

> **Sometimes they have memorial ropings, or maybe a rodeo in memory of the person that died. Sometimes it depends on how popular you are. If you're lucky enough, your hometown might name a rodeo arena after you. We gave away a trophy in memory of dad at the Timber Lake Rodeo.** (*Tater Ward*)

On dates near the anniversary of death, people frequently send pictures or poems to the local newspapers in memory of those who died. The making of memories is an active and creative process, with many ways to keep the memories of loved ones alive. Sometimes prayer, feasts and/or giveaways are held when cemetery headstones have been installed. The tombstone is wrapped in a star quilt and ceremoniously unveiled.

Death is a shocking and disorienting event, but annual memorial rites are a planned and expected part of life. Everyone in the community is touched by death some time. Regularly celebrated times together focus people on the issues of remembering and grieving and promote group solidarity.

SUMMARY

The theological theory of inculturation seeks a dialogue between Christianity and culture which is faithful to both traditions. From the interaction new understandings and rituals emerge. Lakota Catholic culture is an already merged culture, with people drawing from both their Christian and Lakota traditions as they grieve. Practices have emerged in response to a variety of historical influences. This chapter has described current grieving practices from the time that someone dies, through the funeral, until the memorial services which mark the public completion of grieving.

In being with Lakota people during these difficult times, the fundamental values made transparent in and through their cultural rituals are generosity and care for others, especially caring for the *tiyospaye*. These practices speak of a brave and generous people who help one another and build community in the midst of great tragedies. The rituals which teach cultural values and Lakota spirituality are not primarily rituals performed by experts in an overtly religious way. The women who bring pots of soup and the men who shovel dirt on the grave often preach and teach more boldly and clearly than any priest in the pulpit.

Besides expressing appreciation and admiration for the ways Lakota people are present to one another throughout their grieving rituals, this thesis project tries to look critically at the practices. Chapter three examines the dynamics which make it more difficult for these rituals alone to meet grieving Lakota people's needs. Chapter two moves us from an overall descriptive structure of grieving rituals into Lakota people's stories of grieving in relationship to those cultural ways.

Chapter Two

Stories
of
Grieving

My friend, I am going to tell you the story of my life, as you wish; and if it were only the story of my life I think I would not tell it; for what is one man that he should make much of his winters, even when they bend him like a heavy snow? So many other men have lived and shall live that story, to be grass upon the hills. (Black Elk, in Neihardt, p.1)

No story of loss replicates any other . . . you must learn the details of the story each survivor has to tell about how the loss has changed profoundly his or her experience of the world and has limited what is possible in the next chapters of each biography. You must learn the different ways the death disrupts the flow of each survivor's life story. You must learn how each survivor faces distinct challenges and struggles to go on in the next chapters of life (Attig, p. 7).

Having an overview of the basic structure for grieving activities on the Cheyenne River Reservation provides the background for understanding the stories Lakota people have to share about grieving. How do people experience these practices in relation to the deaths in their lives? Each of these stories told by grieving survivors is unique. While very personal, these stories can also speak universal truths not just about pain and sorrow, but also about integrating loss into one's life, remembering, and going onward. Lakota elders speak of the importance of the circle. Each person around the circle of life looks from a unique vantage point. By sharing their experiences and insights, each adds a truth which makes the circle more complete. While unique, you will find in these stories universal themes related to the grieving process.

DEATH AT THE END OF LIFE

We begin with two accounts of the deaths of people who lived full lives, raised families and saw their grandchildren carry on the family line. The first story is of Belle, a wife and grandmother, who died due to complications from diabetes and kidney failure. There is no such thing as a normal death, but Belle's death fits into society's expectations that people die when they are older, die of a disease, and die after the doctors have done all they can to help. *Louis Jewett* grew up in the country near Whitehorse and is retired there now after working in Eagle Butte for the Bureau of Indian Affairs for many years. His wife of forty-seven years, Belle, died in 1994. They have five children, seventeen grandchildren and thirteen great grandchildren.

Belle developed a kidney disorder. That same time she found out she was diabetic. She was being dialyzed for about two and a half years. At that time she got an infection in her toe and it wouldn't heal. From that, she had to have part of her leg amputated. It never would heal right. They had to take another part of her leg off, so they went above the knee. That psychologically affected her and she reached a point where she almost gave up. She had to be moved. She had to be handled. And for a lady that was always handy with everything, a good cook, good to her children, she couldn't do that any more because of her handicap. We were in and out of the hospital up here, Pierre, Eagle Butte, Pierre, Rapid City, started all over again from Pierre to Eagle Butte and then to Pierre. Finally they did take her to Minneapolis.

Every day, she slipped a little bit more. I don't know if you could have noticed it or not, because she's always smiling and being happy. That's how she dealt with it. But me and my children were there every day and we saw. She knew it herself that she wasn't getting any better. The doctor said we'd have to give her up. The way things are right now, the state of health that she's in, it's not for curing, not for getting well, you know. I knew ahead of time. I never did tell my boys, or my granddaughters, but they had

48

an idea that was what was coming up. The doctor said, "It's up to you and your family to go in and humor her and do whatever you can think of to make it easier for her," which we did.

It got to a point where things were not looking very good for her. Everything was going downhill. So she was in the hospital, oh, two months. It was getting awful close to Christmas, so we decided that she'd come home. But she had to stay in the hospital up here at Eagle Butte. The kids all got together and got a Christmas tree for right in the hospital. She come back on a Friday, before Christmas. Sunday we had a little get together with all the kids. We had her presents, all the presents the kids got for her. We got stuff for the grandkids and she was telling them how to open and play with them.

Some people wanted to have an Indian ceremony there for her. So we had a pipe ceremony. They prayed in Lakota, to the North, the East, the South, the West. He lit up the pipe and each person that was present in the circle around the bed all had a chance to smoke a little bit of the pipe, all the way around. It indicated that it would get all evil things away from her soul, so she had a clear way of going to Grandfather (*Tunkasila*). At 9:20 that evening, December 26th, Belle passed away. That was quite a moment for me and my children. They cleared the room and I stayed inside with her alone for a while. Then we talked about arrangements.

With the old Indians, you could always tell when someone had passed away in their family. In the village, early in the morning, they'd take all their possessions, clothes, whatever they had and put them in a neat little pile right on the outside of the tipi.

49

They'd burn it. Burn everything she possessed. Just like smoke goes up in the air like the soul goes to heaven. Traditionally, that's what they did to provide the necessary preparations for their body and soul.

Anyway, it was quite a deal, and we had a lot of clothes. Lot of quilts and blankets she had started. Lots of pieces she had cut up in little squares, all together all in a pile. I decided to go back a few years and I decided to do the same thing traditionally people in the early times did, when they lost one of the family. So we had a burning, down home. I had each grandchild, my two sons and daughters. They each took a pile of clothing and each one would put a piece on the fire and let it burn. Then we'd go around, until we used up all the clothes. The burning of the clothes was not getting rid of it, but the clothes went like she did, going up in the air.

As far as my feelings were concerned, I had to go through a time where I felt like there was an injustice done, kind of feeling sorry for myself and I had self-pity. Another stage was anger. I didn't really get mad at any one in particular. I asked Why? Why did this have to happen to me? Why did this have to happen to my family? As time went on this past year and a half, I'd go back to the self-pity stage. Go back to the anger stage. They were mixed together. One last stage was - don't forget, but let's go on living. Let's go on with our lives. We'll never forget. We'll always remember. Then I'd be reminded. Every time I turn around, I live in the same house where her and I lived for fifteen years. That was our home. There are still things I haven't moved. It's been a year and a half. Now what I do, I go to church on Sunday and make a

weekly cemetery visit on Sunday afternoon.

From third grade on, Louis went away to Catholic boarding school, spending nine months of each year there. He jokes that he thought the Benedictine Fathers were his father! Even though he was not taught much about traditional Lakota ways, he meaningfully reclaimed the ritual of burning the clothes and did it in a way which bonded his family together. The family also prayed a pipe ceremony just before Belle died. Many tribal members are retrieving the traditional ways in a new integration that is personal and meaningful for them. Belle received communion and anointing of the sick as well. For many Lakota Catholics, the rituals are not something they have to choose between, but they accept and practice both. Louis also points out the added trouble that people who live in rural areas have in accessing health care, traveling to doctors many hours away. But he showed how the Indian Health Service hospital served as a hospice for them.

Another type of death which seems more normal and expected, is the death of parents. *Tater* and *Marty Ward* talk about their dad's death. Dick Ward died of a heart attack at home in 1994 at the age of sixty-three. But the death of a second parent can bring memories of an earlier death flooding back. Delores, their mom, died of cancer in 1978. They are two of four brothers who grew up in Whitehorse in a family with strong ranch and rodeo ties. Tater explained, I'm proud to be an Indian, but I have never followed up on the Indian tradition that much. They proudly call themselves cowboys. Both in their thirties, they have families of their own.

Tater: I was 20 years old when my mother died of cancer. I was 36 years old when my father died. He had a massive heart attack. With my mother we knew it was coming. We prayed that it wouldn't come, hoped it wouldn't come, but eventually, cancer got the best of her and took her away from us. With dad, he'd had a few strokes and was in the hospital. The last one got him the best and it took him away from us. It was pretty sudden and was a shock

to all of us.

Marty: Yeah, I remember my mother taking me in the back bedroom and explaining to me what was going on with her. And showing me her breast was gone. That was kind of tough. I was a kid then. When mom passed away, I got to see her the night before. I was only 14 years old then, I went over to the Mobridge hospital and mom told me that she was tired of hanging on and the Good Lord had come to get her. We all sat around there and cried.

Tater: I was away at a rodeo. I come back and went down home there and I got back late. Grandma Ward was there. I said, I'm gonna run over and spend some time with mom. I'd been on the road and she said, 'You look tired. You'd better stay here.' So I did. The next day, my aunt Sharon come and told us that mom had died. I wish I would have went there for a little bit. They always say that when somebody dies and their soul is going to heaven, that it rains. It rained all that next day. Like Marty said, the pain never really goes away. I still grieve even for mom. That's 18 years now. When I start talking about it, I get a lump in my throat. You always know in the back of your mind that they're gone and you ain't got nobody else to turn to, but just the four boys. You gotta hold things together and try to go on with it the best that we can.

I was the first one there when my father died. It was tough to see him as I walked into the house and seen him laying there on the floor. I couldn't do nothing for him. I caught myself feeling angry. Wishing I would have tried to have done more. Wished I'd known about the medical deal. It was hard for me to call my brothers and tell them that our dad had died and find the right words.

Marty: I remember when the cops came to my house, because I didn't have a phone. They told me to call dad's house right away. In the back of my mind I knew that something was wrong. The grieving started right there and then and is still going on, two years now.

Tater: We live out in the country and do a lot of riding. I've always seen eagles, but I've never found an eagle feather in my life. But in between the time dad died and the time we buried him, I was corning cows. I was honking the horn in the pick up waiting for them to come up that hill and I happened to look out the window. There laid a great big long eagle feather. People more up on the Indian traditions said that was a good sign. If you look close on there, it has a white marking. If it was meant to be, it will have something that will remind you of your dad. One of the white markings got a great big cow's head with horns and it looks like it's on there with its tail in the air.

At the wake, sitting up all night with dad was important to me because that was the last that I was going to see of him, for a while, until I hope to meet him and mom. Once they closed the lid on that casket, that was it. I remembered him as being alive, but I wanted to spend as much time with him at the wake as I could. I love him. I miss him.

Marty: Same thing here. Spend every last second. Being there. Looking at him. Then when we took him from Whitehorse to Timber Lake, we went around the house one time.

Tater: We had fed all his cows there by the road early that morning. As we were going along to Timber Lake, J.D. (The funeral director) stopped. It

53

was just like all his cows had quit eating and they all looked at the same time, like they were saying good-bye to the boss. Looking over our way.

Before we walked out of church to go to the cemetery, they held a tape recorder up to the micro-phone and dad was on tape, his version of a cow-boy's prayer. I looked over and I seen a lot of grown men over there crying. Of course I was one of them too. As we left the church that day, to see him to the cemetery us boys got horseback and followed the team and wagon with dad in the back. The pin fell out on the way up and the team about run off, and we was broke down right in front of the rodeo grounds. It was like dad wanted to take one last look, one last stop at the rodeo grounds before he went on to his final resting place. Dad would've probably liked that. We always rode by his side. We always rode down there and helped him ride. We wanted to take one last ride with him.

Marty: I remember saying at the cemetery site, whoever said 'cowboys don't cry was a liar!' (Laughs)

Tater: That's an OK thing because I don't care how tough you think you are, you lose somebody you love, you choke up some time. Whether it be when you're off by yourself, or amongst people. The harder you want to hold it back, the sooner it catch-es up to you. You open a little and weep, and the river runs. About a month after dad died, we buried his brother Bill. I was casket bearer at his funeral. And it was like reliving dad's all over again because it was in the same church.

Marty: I caught myself dialing his number there, a couple of times there right after. I even called it just to let it ring down there.

Tater: About a month after dad had died I was over here doing chores. Down by the arena there's an old tree where he put his mounting pad. I was coming out down below with a tractor. Just as soon as I got straight on with that tree, that tree wasn't there, but there stood dad, just as plain as I see you right now. He had his coveralls on and had a cigarette in his hand, he was really smoking. It was going right up into the sky and he was standing there like he was watching me. Waiting for me to get done. I wasn't scared. I was happy to see him. I kept driving. I wasn't even watching where I was going or anything. I was just watching him, but real fast he went backwards and vanished, and there was that tree again. It wasn't too long after that I was gonna move the round bale feeder to a different spot. It was about an hour after that maybe. Just as I got out of the tractor, I heard him calling my name.

I visit the gravesite quite often. Of course I live the closest. I do a lot of visiting. My kids go to school in Timber Lake, so I stop up there quite often. Say a prayer, talk to both of them. But I did that even with mom, stop up there and talk to her as if she's still alive. Just kind of like visit.

Marty: When I pass through there in my work truck I always stop in. Put a little tobacco out. That's kind of an Indian tradition. They use tobacco when someone dies. I don't know what the deal is there, but I know my wife's family they always leave food out, leave it towards the east. I went to my wife's auntie's funeral. I didn't know her that good, but when someone would come up to my wife and cry around and grieve, I could feel myself swelling up with feeling. But to be strong for my wife, I had to cowboy up and hold it back in.

Tater: If a person dies that you're close to, like your father or your mother, you're hurting, you're grieving but there's all these people around so you feel a little better. But when everything's all done and over with, and you got all that quiet time to yourself, that's when it's tough. Because you ain't got nobody there to talk to, or visit with about something else. You got all that thinking time. You miss them. You wish that they was with you. That's when the grieving really starts, when the funeral is all over with and you got all this time to yourself.

It was tough enough for me losing our parents, but it was also the loss of my kids' grandfolks. With me, they've only got one grandma left. They don't see them that often. Like with dad, they are getting to that age where they can go help him round up, go help him ride and stuff. He liked that. I tried to tell my kids all I can about not only my dad, but about my mother. Troy's kids, they're all young and they didn't know grandpa Dick or Grandma Delores. A lot of that was taken away from them. Dad's place will always be home, but you go over there and, I used to stop, have coffee, visit and have a lot of laughs. Now you go over there, sit and look around, think about the old times. It's been two years. For me as time goes on, I remember more of the happier times. I guess you try not to think of the bad. But you try to think of the good times we've had.

A significant group of tribal members are cowboys/ranchers. They are often unfamiliar with traditional Lakota religious practices. But visions like the one Tater described and signs like the eagle feather are still a part of their reality. Marty knew the traditional practice of offering food and tobacco at the gravesite. Although not knowing why he did that, he still found meaning in the ritual. Their dad's death brought back memories of their mother, and when the same extended family gathered a month after Dick's death, to bury his brother Bill, they were faced with many of the same feelings and emotions all over again.

Tater and Marty explain how incorporating their cowboy way of doing things was important at the funeral. Marty spoke of how cowboys surely cry, but he also spoke of the expectation to cowboy up and suffer the pain quietly, being strong and tough. When it comes to grieving, people receive many mixed messages about what they should or should not do.

While Dick Ward died at the age of sixty-three, Delores died before her family was raised. Appendix Four shows that 59% of the deaths in the Aberdeen IHS Service Area are people under the age of sixty-five. The deaths of younger people complicates grieving for survivors.

WHEN DEATH DISRUPTS

These next stories are organized around three ways that death disrupts:

Tragic or traumatic death - a frequent occurrence on the reservation, which can leave survivors feeling angry and thinking that they were cheated. Many use the phrase, they died before their time, in such situations.

Conflicted death - when unresolved issues of anger or guilt are directed toward the deceased. Survivors may not have a strategy for addressing those issues.

Multiple Loss - when survivors are dealing with more than one death, or they have not worked through the tasks grieving requires from a previous death. A broader sense of loss which includes things like the loss of culture and the death of hopes also emerges.

You will find that these disruptions can overlap. Some of the stories reflect all three types.

TRAUMATIC DEATH

Tragic or traumatic deaths can leave people feeling overwhelmed by intense emotions and unanswerable questions. One of the most difficult deaths to accept is the death of a child. *Debbie Day* is a rancher and the community health representative from the Bridger community. She speaks of the death of her eighteen-year-old son Ryan, who died in an accidental shooting.

Ryan always checked cattle and he decided to hunt prairie dogs. That night, about 11:30, I knew, as a mother, I sensed that there was something wrong. I know my Ryan. He wasn't the type that would leave the four wheeler and run off. Wherever he goes, we know. But he wasn't back on time. At three o'clock in the morning they found him and they told me that he was gone. That night I completely lost it. It was really hard on me. For all of us. And I almost blamed my husband Kenny for buying that gun. But you see, I wasn't thinking clearly. I was blaming. And Kenny was hurt too, like I was. But them couple three hours, I was completely not myself.

I was arguing in my mind with God. I asked God Why'd you allow this? Why? Why did it happen to an innocent, to such a good boy? He always goes to church. He always chose the right thing. Band player, respected girlfriend. Why did he have to have a tragic death? Why did this happen to him, God? Where were you? Where was the guardian angel? Why?

It took me a long time to really see the death as an accident. It was terrible. My inner voice told me I shouldn't be blaming. Because accidents happen. And yet deep inside, I want to blame and I hold it. I lost Ryan and I was upset. I just did not think I could go on as a mother for all my other children and

58

grandchildren. I guess that's because we put Ryan first, always. For everything. Because we had everything planned out for Ryan. To take care of our son Dustin, who is handicapped. To run the place. Keep our place. I was looking for grandchildren. I wanted him to have a right person to marry and have a wedding. As a mother, you think of those things. He was in the sports, he was in all choir singing in Rapid, he goes to the rodeo. Actually he made us really proud. So I couldn't deal with that, his death. Losing everything. And it took me a while. At first I blamed. I forgot everybody. God even. I took it so hard that I blew up before everybody. I thought nobody cared, or nobody would grieve with me. Sr. Inez came from Rapid and brought me right back to reality. I really have to hold on and get myself together. And I knew that as much as I was hurt, I'm sure that God is hurt too. So I thought, well, I'd better get my faith back together in God. Be strong for the whole family.

I thought to myself, I'll handle my crying alone, when nobody sees me. And that's what I do. I pray and I cry. I put myself grieving, with what Mary went through. I usually talk about what she went through, when they were hanging Jesus on the cross.

All the school kids in Faith High School, they went through so much. They put roses on his grave, and one of the high school girls made a plaque for his grave. Walking with Christ - Ryan Day. And they had a football homecoming. All the field goals with his number, 66. They made a pin that had #66 Ryan Day on it. They had a parade and they made a float for him. Things like that, I cried, that I had a son like him. About 500 people attended the funeral, which filled the Faith High School.

I still have all his stuff. I did manage to release some. But I feel that he is still with me. I mean I still got his car and I talk to him, as I talk to God. I still go to his grave. I just go out there and I talk to him and I feel relieved when I do that.

Used to be when I saw young boys with black hats on, I feel like crying, and then I get a little jealous.

I had that funeral and the giveaway for him. This is what I wanted to do for him. I fulfilled that promise to Ryan and I feel relieved. When you have a giveaway for a loved one, you put it all behind them. So that's why I wanted to give away.

And people were also saying that I was kind of a bad person, so God punished me, or took my son away. You know, - he had a tragic death, out of warning. And that hurt me very much. They were saying that she better live to humble herself, - things like that. But why would God destroy a person he created? He wouldn't do that.

Dustin says, You know mother, I wonder when will I die so I can see my brother? I said, That we don't know. But, I said, someday. You don't want to die. You've got a lot of things to do on this earth. You can't just stay there. When you grieve, you have to go on. And after a year, we have to live for ourselves. I'm sure if I was to die tomorrow, I'd want them to continue. Sure, we miss them if something happens. We miss them and we cry. But I said, we'll see each other. We have to go on with our lives and I said if we work it right, while on this earth we'll see Ryan.

If you lose a loved one, it's terrible. You think everything is over. But you think of those others,

like if you have other children, or your husband, and go on, and always have faith in God.

Accidental deaths with no explanation can leave unanswerable questions. Looking for someone or something to blame is common. At first Debbie took her anger out on her family and on God. A child's death puts tremendous strain on the spouses' relationship. Debbie also shared the harsh words coming from people she had been feuding with that blamed her for the death. Such conflicts unrelated to the loss get attached to the grieving and demand careful pastoral attention.

The activities of talking to those who have died and experiencing their ongoing presence are a strong part of Lakota culture. Other stories which follow reflect this experience of the deceased person's spirit.

Ryan's funeral was held at Faith High School and the 500 people who attended the funeral equals the entire population of Faith. Especially when school aged children die, the funerals become public events and ministers need to be aware of the death's impact on the entire community.

Doris Hump reflects on the shooting death of her brother, which also brings back memories of her father's death as well. Doris is from the Red Scaffold community and works at the Takini school kitchen.

My dad died on July 26, 1972 and my brother died April 17, 1977. I'm still grieving. I don't think that's ever going to go away. That's always part of myself. Now that I start talking about them, it's like it just happened yesterday. I really get emotional about it. But I know that I'll never get over grieving for them. My older brother died in a tragic way and it's really hard for me. I never even thought he was gonna die like that. He's just a year older than me and I always looked up to him for everything after my dad passed away. When my brother was gone, then there was nobody and I didn't know what to do. In this whole world full of people, I never felt so alone.

From there on I was just starting to learn to be

61

responsible myself. I remembered their words and that's what helped me through. Like all the advice that they gave. They always say God works in mysterious ways. That's one of them. That He allowed me to know Him so that I could pray to Him, ask for guidance, so I can go through these things. I pray for my dad and my brother. You're supposed to pray for the dead because they can't do it anymore, because you're supposed to be praying and doing all those things when you're still living on earth. Once we pass earth and go on, then you can't do those things. So that's what I do. I pray for my relatives or anybody. When I pray for my dad and my brother, I can picture them being happy and moving even closer to the Lord.

Even though they're dead, they're still a part of me, because I can't forget them. People talk to you, at the time of their death, comforting you with their words. I heard a lot of them say, It's gonna take time, but you'll forget, and you're gonna go on with your life. Yeah, I'm gonna go on with my life, but I'm not gonna forget. I can't forget. I'm gonna be grieving as long as I live.

It was really hard because I looked up to them for everything. That's what I keep telling my girls. You have to start taking responsibility. When I mention death, well then they don't want me to talk about death. I always tell them that's part of life. You have to talk about death, or you're gonna run into trouble. I say, You have to know these things because what if all of a sudden I died? Mom, please don't say that. Mom don't say you're gonna die. I said, You've got to know these things. That's why I'm saying them.

Duane's best friend was Presley Circle Eagle. He

even used to stay with us a lot. He was just like part of the family. The girls really took to him and they were really close to him. They used to call him *lala* (grandfather) Pres. Mom, I had a dream about *lala* Pres. He was asking me what I wanted. They really felt a big loss there. If they dream, I tell them to just pray for him. Then they feel better. A lot of times when they tell me about their dream, I can tell that they really miss him.

My mom and dad never did talk to me about death. My dad tried, but the only way he got the courage to talk like that was when he was drinking. And so we never paid attention.

My brother graduated from college. And then he came back to work on the reservation as an accountant for this one program. That happened in Faith. They said he shot himself, but my sister said that the cop, the one that beat up Calvin Knife, was there. I don't know the real story and I don't even want to know.

My brother had a pistol. My sister bought a pistol. I didn't know why she did. He was in the pickup. They said he pulled it out from under the seat and then he shot himself. That friend told that cop, Don't you think you should call the ambulance? He said, Oh, he's just another Indian. He's gonna die anyway! The friend ran, and it was late, so he had a hard time getting into that mall. That bartender opened up and he ran in there and called that ambulance. When that ambulance came, he was still conscious. They put him in the ambulance. I don't know what that cop said to my brother, but my brother dug into his pocket and he threw all his change at him and said, Here's the rest of my money. From him moving around like that, that bullet went and lodged in his brain and that's when he went unconscious. He never did come to. We were in the hospital when he passed away. We couldn't stay in his room, but they just let us in there, for a little time, to hold his hand. I said, We're going to wait for you. He really squeezed my hand. But he died right after that. I know that he heard me.

They always say that when they die their spirit leaves them, and that spirit goes back to the place where they love to be. I know that's true because when my brother was there in the hospital my mother stayed home. My younger brother came after her, to take her. But she didn't want to go. She said she knew. She said she had a feeling. Nobody told her, but she knew already. She said she heard him sit down on his bed and lay down on his bed. She said that was his spirit.

On decoration day, I get over, clean the grave, put flowers, food, and I sit there and I talk to them. I always ask them, Why?

Is the task of grieving to forget or to remember? Doris points out that grieving is a life long process. As a mother, she sees the importance of talking honestly about death with her children, even when there is resistance. Doris shows the Lakota value of being with the dying person and also gives a glimpse into the Lakota conviction that spirits do not die with death.

Ronnie's death occurred against a background of racial tension that is all too real. Traumatic deaths may lead people to be obsessed about discovering the details of how the person died. On the other hand, Doris said she did not want to know. Knowing what happened may be as painful in some cases as not knowing, especially with the possibility the person took their own life. *Chuck LeCompte* grew up on a ranch outside Ridgeview and is a police officer now living in Eagle Butte. He tells the story of his son Rick's shooting death, where discovering the details became a primary concern.

Late one night the phone rang and they wanted me to come up to the jail to get Rick. He'd had a fight with his wife. I was kind of grouchy, but I woke up and went to the jail. I talked to a couple of the police officers that were there. They said, There are no charges on him and he can go, but he has to stay away from his house. He has to stay at your house. So we loaded up and got home and I said, I'm going back to bed, but you can stay on the couch here.

In the morning when I got up he was gone. Later the phone rang again. It was Rick's wife Gayle, telling me to go over at the house, because they can't find Rick. She said, Go over there, because he's got that gun. And just like that I got a funny feeling in my stomach. Like I knew what I was gonna find before I got there.

I walked over there. I was still in the garage and I reached up and knocked on the door. No answer, so I stepped up on the porch and I looked through the window and I did see him on the middle of the floor. There was a little bitty red spot on his back. And I thought, Oh no! I looked inside the house and seen if there was anything splattered before I went in. Really terrible. I tried the door and it was open. So I just walked in. And I could see that he was dead already. He was laying on his face. I walked over to him. I remember looking around in the house. But I really can't be positive I seen that gun. And it kind of bothers me. Because if I didn't see a gun, then where did the gun come from when the police officers got there?

As a police officer, I walked into real tragic things

- where the people shot their heads off. I've always managed to look around before I went in but on that, I just went right in. I didn't look around like I should have. There should have been an autopsy done, but there wasn't. I'm still kind of mad at myself because I didn't go in as a police officer. I should have let the police officer part of me take over. That was my work. I shouldn't have went in. If I would have done that, maybe there would have been a better investigation. I don't know if I'll ever quit doubting.

I guess I really can't describe the feelings that I had then. I just thought Why! Why? I think that what bothered me the most, was that I didn't sit up with him that night. If I'd have sat up with him, then he wouldn't have left. I tried to keep myself busy, all during that time, I thought of things to do. I shoveled on a whole pickup load full of corn, all by hand. I just felt bad that we couldn't have spent more time together. I thought of all the times that I hurt him.

It kind of seems like people stayed away from me. I really don't know why. There were people coming to the house. I guess I expected more. I got blamed for a lot of things. My ex wife Dallas said I spent so much time chasing down other people's kids, but I neglected my own. When I went back to the DARE program, if I thought of something else, I could talk. I didn't want to talk about that. When I first went back to the schools, I told the principal, before the class even started, that I was not very comfortable, worried they might say or ask something about it.

I took the trash out one day. And my wife Sharon was watching. I went to put it in the dumpster, turned around and walked back. And when I came in the house, she said, who was that guy beside the house? What guy? You had to see him. You walked right by him! You know, like that. Dallas and my daughter Mona, they both said they'd seen him; he walked around the house. But I never did.

The anniversary of his death, I thought about him all day. And that night I didn't know if I was dreaming, or what. But it was like he come in the door. And then I got up, I was just down the hall and I said, Who is it? Just about then, somebody came out of the room where he used to sleep all the time. I put my overshoes on and I followed him down the hallway. Just as soon as he got out in the hallway, he sat down on the couch. I walked over to him and I was hugging him. I don't know. I'd like to say I was, he was in the house. I dreamt I wanted to give him a hug. I guess I did. So much more I could have did for him. I miss him a lot. I got a habit of keeping things to myself. Sharon chews me out about it every now and then. You know, if I don't tell her something.

He used to come and drink coffee in the morning. Just about every morning. I miss that. Talked about things we were going to do. I think about him, especially the wrestling program. Every time I go to the gym, I can see him out on the floor. When I hear the song Jingle Bells, Rick comes to my mind, every time.

I asked Chuck how it would be if they had done an autopsy and found no doubt that Rick had shot himself. That's probably what I'm scared of, he said. Suicide is hard to accept. He found himself doubting and feeling guilty for not staying up with Rick that night and for not doing more with Rick as he was growing up. This raises a second theme which impacts grieving.

CONFLICTED GRIEVING

Conflicted or unresolved grieving in the relationship with the one who died can take many forms. Chuck mentioned guilt, and at times dwelled on the ways he might have hurt his son. Other conflicts arise out of alcohol influenced behavior, all too common among families on Cheyenne River. *Doris Hump* spoke of how difficult it was to talk with her father or take seriously what he had to say when he was drinking. Physical, emotional or sexual abuse may accompany the drinking (and also occur independently of any alcohol abuse). *Peggy Knife* tells about her brother's suicide. The conflict she felt was with her deep religious belief that suicide is a sin, which made it so important for her to have the chance to pray for forgiveness before her brother died. Peggy lives in Red Scaffold and works with the Head Start Program. A convert to Catholicism, she went through the Ministry Formation Program with her husband *Ted*, who is a Roman Catholic Deacon.

One of the hardest deaths in my family was the death of my little brother. My brother's death was harder than my dad's. The reason why, maybe it was because you know when they're older they're going to die eventually. But you don't expect that when they're young. I was like a mother to the younger ones. We kind of grew up poor, like a lot of us Indian people in Red Scaffold. We always had food to eat, but still, we didn't get to have a lot of other things, like, we grew up without electricity and running water. I wanted a good life. I always wanted things to be better for them.

When my little brothers were drinking, I worried about them a lot. I just prayed for their safety. When they were drinking anything could happen, a car accident, a fight, violence. I was always worried about them. My littlest brother was really shy. I think that's why he took to drinking because then he was able to talk to people and do things that he couldn't

68

do when he was sober. All his friends drank too, so he went out and partied whenever he got a chance on weekends. Here he ended up staying with a girl in Dupree. He was drinking and she called the cops on him. Within an hour he hung himself.

We got the message that they revived him and flew him to Bismarck. All this time I kept praying, Don't let him die. I want to pray with him. When we got there, I really felt for him and when I saw him I said, In your mind, just ask Jesus' forgiveness and at that moment, he will forgive you. Don't forget. I want you to do that, in your heart. I really talked to him and I told him about the scriptures. I knew he heard me because he had tears in his eyes.

When they told me he had passed away, I just couldn't even bear to tell my folks. It was really hard on the whole family. When that happened, I didn't feel like eating for about five days. I just went through the motions of going back to work. I didn't talk to people. I didn't care what happened in the past, I didn't even care about the future. That moment! Hard to get through that moment. I was working in Eagle Butte and I stayed up here at my mom's house during the week. I wasn't usually with my husband Ted all the time, but he stayed up here because I wanted him beside me all the time. But yet when I was with him, I was like, in my own world. I couldn't even hardly talk. But I wanted him beside me.

When we went through the funeral, it was like being in a daze. We knew we had to get stuff ready and we did all that, but nobody started crying. We all went out to Rapid and bought giveaway stuff. We had people sewing star quilts, getting a cow ready.

Ted did that. We all went to the funeral home together. We bought new clothes for him. Our whole family went down. So we went through all of that and it was hard, but there were just things we had to do. So we worked until we got it done.

At that wake, I don't even remember what they said. I heard some of it, but most of the time my mind was on him. Later on after the funeral and everything was over, we were up here, all I could think of was what happened that weekend. I just didn't care anymore. All the things I cared about just went out the window. I just didn't even care. I was thinking, why did I ever worry about all the stuff in the past? It doesn't even matter. Time doesn't matter, it's just this moment that matters. If I could just get through this moment. It was like living from moment to moment.

About a month after that, we went out to a retreat. I thought I was going to get to talk to one of the priests about this, and here, when I started to cry, he just kind of cut me off, like he didn't want to hear anything like that. So I thought, I'd better not cry. I tried not to cry after that. I kept everything in after that. I didn't want to talk to anybody.

I really got hooked on pow wows because I could just forget about everything. Just sit there and concentrate on that pow wow and watch people. I didn't have to think about it. I wanted to go to pow wows every weekend. It helped me forget.

What gave me hope, something to look forward to, was the giveaway. We had to get ready for the memorial dinner. It was hard work, but I looked forward to nothing else but that. That's what kept me going too. I'd start thinking about that. Getting

ready for that.

In many reservation families, children like Peggy often take on parent-like responsibilities for brothers, sisters and other relatives. This intensifies emotional bonds and complicates grieving. Peggy repressed her tears after feeling cut off by a priest when she started to cry, which started her on a pattern of shutting down her feelings. Peggy's story is a reminder that the way we respond to tears and emotions has enormous impact to help or hinder the grieving process.

Peggy got hooked on pow wows to numb her pain, while other people find their escape in gambling, alcohol and other addictions. Some jump from one destructive relationship to another. Peggy describes the strong grief emotions, the ambivalence of wanting to be close and wanting distance, and feeling stuck in the moment of remembering the death, all of which led her to withdraw from others and stuff her feelings inside. The cultural rituals, however, helped bring her out of the withdrawal and avoidance. The rituals of grieving gave her something to work for and a reason to keep going onward.

I will come back to Peggy a little later, but the third theme which emerges from people's experience is how many of them are grieving for more than one person at the same time.

MULTIPLE LOSS

Iyonne Garreau was raised in Whitehorse and has lived in Eagle Butte for the past 20 years. She directs the elderly nutrition program. Talking about her husband Ellsworth's death brought back memories of so many other deaths that touched her family.

I remember Mona, my older sister that died of tuberculosis. She began to hemorrhage when she was playing basketball. So they took her home and then right from there they took her to the Sanitarium. She stayed there until she died. My father was so devoted. He went to Rapid City. He got a job so he could be there with her, throughout that whole year and a half, two years. That was the first one for mom

and dad. I was young then, around 8 or 9. I just followed my mother around, crying when she did.

After that, when they lost Blueie, one of the
twins, that was horrid. That was so horrible for all of
us. He was missing in action in Korea. My brother
Pinkie got the telegram. My grandmother said something in Indian. She just screamed. I never heard her
do that before. But she delivered the babies when
they were born, the little twins. She just thought the
world of them. My father, I remember him just break-
ing up completely. He went up on the hill where my
grandpa is buried. You could see him walking back
and forth. My mom, the fact that she never could
bury him, she just claimed the unknown soldier's
grave. When my dad went to Washington the last
time, she sold her cow so she could go with my dad.
She spent a lot of time at the Unknown Soldier's
Grave, because that was the closest to a graveyard
or cemetery or a tombstone that she'd ever have.

Orlin dying. He was killed in a car accident. That
too was so terrible! I don't know if mom was ever
really the same. It just seemed like after a while God
just let her mind be the way it was, because she
couldn't cry anymore. They went through so much.
But they found a strength, I don't know. We were
there for mom and dad. But we hurt so much.

When my husband Ellsworth died, I never really
had time to really get into my grief because that first
year that Ellsworth was gone, these kids were taking
me out to dinner, they were taking care of me. The
second year was when I really, really missed him. I
wanted to be alone a lot. If I wanted to cry and holler,
I did those things! All by myself. Nobody knows
about it. But the second year was when I really griev-

ed for my husband. There was so much in home care. It was like I was waiting for a year and a half for him to die. They told me he doesn't have more than six months to live. And in six months, he was going and going and going. It was a year and a half after that he finally died. He messed up all the doctors! When he wasn't moving in bed, I'd have to shake the bed to make sure he wasn't dead. I feared even using the word dead, die, anything. Finally, I can do that now. We didn't even talk die, dead, pass away, nothing! Never would face the fact that he was gonna leave. We knew more than ever that we weren't going to have him, but we never - it was just like if we talked about it, it was gonna happen.

One time they had to use those paddles to revive him. Afterwards, he said, You know what I was going through? I was walking and it looked like there was someone ahead of me. And the sky was blue, just beautiful. And he's not one for anything, words like that. But he said, It was just beautiful. You know, I didn't want to come back. But he heard somebody holler. You see that was doctor, and that must have been me. Toward the end, he went back to that. He feared nothing.

It was Good Friday and he began to have all these little rattles. They told me there would be a death rattle. There's absolutely the truth to that, because your body begins to shut down, then noth- ing is working. So there's gonna be some sounds and some weird things that are going on. He made sure I had finished the dresses for those two little granddaughters, because he just cared for them so much. Sarah and Diana. So they put on their new dresses. They paraded in front of him, Easter

73

Sunday morning. Five minutes to five on Easter he was gone. Just left. No facial expressions, no nothing. He just closed his eyes. He was too young to die, 63. But he did. I would never in my entire life put myself in a situation, of being married to another person. Because I don't want to feel a part of me dying anymore.

I still miss him. I still am angry sometimes, when I wish he would have told me something. There's just things that we took each other for granted - so much that I'd forget to ask him. Why didn't I ask him about that? There's a lot of things that I don't know yet that I should have. We should have talked more. It makes me angry because now there's no way. It was so stupid of me to not have visited about whatever.

That man hasn't left me every day ever since he died. Never. It's every day that I think about something. What I wanted to have of him afterwards was just all the pictures I could gather up. I was sorry that we never even took a family picture. You don't think about those things when everybody is doing OK. We talk about him. Something is always coming up. He's always a part of us - especially at gatherings. We'll always talk about him.

His big brother and dad dying on the same day. We went through that. We lost a little baby together and I remember how we went through that. Mary Beth was her name. She's buried down in Whitehorse. We went through that together. That's when I started to work. I needed to get out and work, because I was just skin and bones. I had health problems. I don't know why. She was just a little baby, you never even seen her. Didn't even look at her. The kids didn't even see her. Little casket, that's all. I don't know why I would have sunk into that depression. It seems I should have been a little stronger than that. My whole life changed after that. The doctor said, You need to work and to do something. Prior to that, that's all I did was take care of my children. I did whatever I was supposed to do. I began to work and I liked it. And I haven't stopped working since.

A granddaughter died. When that baby died, Diane, it just broke her up, losing one of those little kids. When you start putting all the deaths in sequence I guess it could add up to quite a story.

Adding up all the losses, it is quite a story. Two brothers and a sister, a daughter and granddaughter died before reaching the age of 25. On average 15% of the population on Cheyenne River die before the age of 25. (USDHHS 1996a) Iyonne's experience of grieving the loss of people too young to die is repeated many times on the reservation.

People can experience loss in many ways. Lakota people speak of an historical or inherited grief they carry, due to their losses of language, culture and land. *Rosie Roach Avery* is a teacher, mother and grandmother, living in the Red Scaffold community. She mentions the deaths of two brothers, one who died in a car wreck, the other in Vietnam. Rosie also names some of the other, cultural losses, and describes the helping response of the community when others are grieving.

For myself, I went through boarding school. So I didn't have that family with me every day. With the whole process of grieving, you need to be real complete with that person who has gone on. If you're not, I think you just kind of carry that with you. Like with my mom, she's been gone probably 20 years and I never got to really tell her, Mom, I love you and I appreciate that you gave me birth. I never got to tell her that. So what I did, was I had my friend Edie, and

75

I said, Edie, could you be my mom? Because I need to complete with her. So she sat down beside me in this chair and I said, Mom, I never got to tell you, and I really love you and I thank you for giving me birth. And she said, OK my girl, and then we hugged it was just a real awesome experience. It was like my whole head went in a circle. Wow Edie, if I wasn't sitting down, I think I would have been knocked down! It was something that made it complete with my mom. I felt really good. We need to do that with the ones that we have lost.

Like I've lost brothers, one in Vietnam, one in a car wreck and I've never got to tell them those things. For me, I haven't completed that. I need to do that somehow. The brother I lost in Vietnam, it was just like, You didn't have to be over there! Why would you send somebody off to go and to kill innocent people? is what I was thinking. For him not to come home - he did come home, but he was in a casket! I probably still have that with me because I never really completed that. It makes you really think about how you should cherish that person, while they're still alive. So I do that now, with my brothers. I'm not afraid to tell them I love them and when I see them to hug them, stay real open with them and communicate with them, giving my fullest in that relationship with them.

I was taught that it was OK to talk about the ones who died because then you were remembering them. Maybe you haven't seen people for a long time, you might sit down and start talking them, start telling stories about them, remembering them and the things that they did in their life. During the funeral gatherings we've always talked about that person.

Kind of memorialize them while this was all going on.

Even now the names are given to the younger ones as they are being born to carry forth those names. Handed down. It depends on within your family how much of the traditional ways you keep. You hang on to the old traditional names and you give them to your kids. With grief you really have to look at not necessarily just the family unit, you have to look at the extended family unit. Everybody gets involved in that relationship. From there, it reaches out into the community, because there's more relatives, and it gets even bigger, across the reservation.

Getting stuck in grief can happen. It's part of your history. I think about the ways our people were suppressed. I still have that in me and I don't want that. I hope that never happens to myself or to the kids. I hope that I have a say in how I want my life and my children's life to be. Some of the terrible things that you read about and hear about from your dad or grandparents, what they went through. All the really hard times. You get strength from it too. The grieving is in there and at the same time we can get strength from that. My dad, they talk about Wounded Knee, his relatives, how it was for his mom. How they got away from there, they walked and walked clear up into Canada to get away from that! Wow, you know they walked that far! When you really think about those things, if someone has told you that through the history, you just have that in you. When I talk about it, all of a sudden it will just come to me and I get really emotional and I'll be crying. Say a thing like our language and our culture - when we were growing up and our parents were growing up and grandparents were growing up they wanted to do

**away with it. So if it comes down from my grandpar-
ents to my parents and to myself and all the way
down, it's unresolved. It's a big responsibility on me
to make sure that it's never suppressed, that it continues. So I have to do everything that I can to insure
that our language and our culture, all of that, continues.**

I asked Rosie where she learned about the process of completing that
she used with Edie and she replied that she had learned of it from a work-
shop. Lakota tradition is a continual evolving tradition, showing the ability to use new materials and processes.

Rosie also mentioned her loss of being with family during her boarding school experience. Many tribal members from Cheyenne River
attended boarding schools, either government run schools on the reservation, or church run schools off the reservation. Even today, the BIA
staffs dorms in Eagle Butte, where children as young as first grade live
while attending school. People's experience of boarding away from home
has been a mixed one. Some carry emotional scars and traumatic memories. Others found a nurturing environment. Many families had no other
choice than to board their children due to the vast distances they lived
away from a school. Some children boarded because their families
couldn't provide for them at home.

Iyonne Garreau's recounting of Ellsworth's near death vision and the
comfort it brought him as death approached, touches on the issue of culture these histories raise. Lakota people pay close attention to dreams
and visions. Their worldview, which includes a strong belief in the spirit
world will influence their way of grieving.

THE CULTURAL CONTEXT OF DEATH

Lakota persons bring their unique spirituality and cultural worldview to
the grieving process. This is especially evident when people freely speak
of their experiences with dreams and spirits. A third cultural issue I was
only made aware of from these interviews was the understanding of
habits which develop and are imprinted during the four days following a

death.

Suzie Eagle Staff is a social worker in Eagle Butte, who is a practitioner of traditional Lakota cultural ways. She reflects on her brother's funeral and how those traditional ways helped her grieving.

The way we handled the arrangements in our cultural way was with a saging, and the pipe ceremony. It helped me through what was taking place. My brother, the one that passed away, was the one that brought us closer to our ways, our cultural beliefs. It helped me deal with my grief in a good way. I accepted his death to a point, but yet I pray a lot about it.

We did grow up with alcoholism in our family. I basically kind of became a parent after my father passed away. I started taking care of my older sisters and my little brother. My mother is recovering and she's proudly survived. And so have I, and of course, my brother Bob. There was a bonding between all three of us. Working through recovery, we became stronger in our spiritual beliefs. And we removed alcohol and drugs from our lives. So we try to teach our kids these things.

My oldest brother Tom, went to Washington and got my brother and brought him back to South Dakota. Our grieving began with the actual viewing the body. I was asked to smudge my brother Bob. It was just like a purification. But there was still disbelief that he was gone.

With our spiritual beliefs we know we have him, not physically, but spiritually. He's still with us. We believe in that. In grieving that really helps us - knowing that all things are living in one way or another.

It's kind of hard now, and I'm working. I try to put

myself into my job and at the end of the day I'm totally exhausted. I want to go home for supper and this and that. I usually try to go to my room and keep to myself and try to unwind and just meditate. A cultural way that helps currently, is that you cannot do public activities. A lot of times we stay home and we do family activities. And that's really helpful. The extended family is always asking, one way or another. Checking on my mom, checking on how they're doing. I find that helpful.

When they finally brought my brother's body back, his girlfriend wanted to get him dressed and fix his hair. She did, and I helped her. We braided his hair. It was really hard. But I'm glad I did that. It was a reality. What they normally do is that in order to help us to deal with our grief, we view the body and know that he is actually gone. There's no more life in the body. Those that are cremated, you don't know if they're gone or not. The pain is still there, but you don't know. You know there's something in it, but you don't know if it's the person that passed away. Cremation would have been harder for us to really deal with, if he wasn't physically there. What helps the grieving, at the wake service, is staying there all night. A lot of the elderly stayed up all night with the body. I didn't do that with my father, but I did it with my brother. I felt I didn't want to leave him. I think it was good, but yet it was difficult.

We ended his burial with another ceremony that hasn't been done in a long time. And that's the releasing of his spirit. We used cloth and tobacco and a ritual that goes along with it. It's knowing our roots.

In our beliefs if you cry a lot, continue to cry and

not know why you are crying, you can get lost in that. In our belief, if you cry too much, continually, we believe we hold on to them, we don't let him go. The crying is reaching out to them. We want them here, yet we can't let go. And some of the elderly really have a problem with that.

My niece chose to cut her hair as a sign of grieving, but we didn't ask her if she knew what she was gonna be getting herself into. She dances. She gave up dancing but she found it hard to do that. And basically you give up something for the year. But we probably should have stopped her and said, Can you do this for the year, when you give up?

There's a lot of Native Americans that know their culture, but yet they don't know about or quite understand the grieving process over all, whether it be in their own cultural way, unless they actually have it shown to them. A lot of families, now basically, have so much alcoholism that they've seen their parents and grandparents deal with the grief that way. And they were told not to cry. Where that came from I don't know, but that's what they did. They use the alcohol to just numb the pain. And so once a person begins to do that the process is halted, because the person's always numb, and they aren't ever really ready to deal with the grief until they remove the alcohol from their family system. With a lot of people there's confusion about how to deal with their emotions. They're extremely emotional all the time without knowing why.

If you can finish you should finish. When you're thinking about the alcoholism, you start something and not finish it and then you don't feel. You start grieving, but once he's buried, the grieving stops,

81

**and if you try to move on from it you get stuck. It
makes you feel bad, but they just deny it.**

**My father, he had knowledge of the cultural
ways. But I never questioned him. I'd always
observe what he was doing, but he never actually got
us together and started teaching us those ways. And
none of us questioned why they never taught us
about our culture. I did raise the question with my
mom and she said, Well, you never asked. So they
expected us to ask rather than just giving it to us.**

Lakota culture expects grieving persons to pull away from extra activities and spend more time at home with family. Suzie found that made a
positive contribution to her grieving. The direct contact in helping prepare
her brother's body for burial was hard, but helpful. Suzie also points out
the strong belief in and experience of the spiritual presence of the one
who has died. This aided her grieving as well. Another way people experience the presence of the dead is through dreams.

DREAMS

Peggy and Ted Knife say that dream and vision experiences are common and normal for most Lakota people. They are a strong part of their
cultural reality. They share some of their experiences and how they
reacted to them.

**Peggy: I had a dream about my brother and
that's when I started healing. In my dream we were
in this white car and I was sitting in the back seat.
Ted was standing there. And here my little brother
was in the back and he said 'Where's Peggy?' And
Ted said, She's right there, and he pointed at me. I
was thinking, wherever he was at he must be eating
good because he put on some weight! And here he
came and he grabbed me and I grabbed him, and that
was the end of my dream. That was the first dream I
ever had of him. Everybody else was dreaming**

about him, but I never did. That was my first dream about him.

I grew up hearing about those things because my mom and dad believed in those things and my grandparents did too. I had my own personal experience when I was about 18. I was up here with one of my friends. Her boyfriend died in an accident right before that. She wanted me to stay with her because she was feeling really bad and crying. We took her mom to work and then we went back and we slept on her mom's bed. Her little girl slept in the middle and I was on the outside. I was laying there praying and here I opened my eyes and here I saw this man standing right at the foot of the bed. It was just like from the knees on up. I was thinking, am I really seeing this, or is it just my imagination? So I closed my eyes and opened them again and he was still standing there. I guess I really hollered. I didn't want to look again after that, then finally I looked again and he was gone. But this man had on Wranglers and a blue shirt and a black hat, and was just standing there smiling. I didn't know who it was. I don't know why I saw that. My mom would say that if we see someone then something's gonna happen. But nothing happened. I thought that maybe this was her boyfriend that came. That's what I thought.

My little nephew, 18 now, he just had an accident two weekends ago. He said, 'I was going to this place that I'm supposed to go to and I got there and here I saw Grandma Eunice.' Our grandma, she just died a couple months ago. He said he saw her there and she told him to come back because he's not supposed to be there yet. 'So I came back. She got me back. She told me to get to the road and stand and wait because my cousin Ford is supposed to come and pick me up.' And here that's who came. That's who found him. And they didn't even know he wrecked because he didn't tell them nothing. He just got in. He said 'Grandma was standing there waiting so I waved at her and then they brought me back.'

I still pray for all of my ancestors every day when I say my rosary. I pray for their souls.

Ted: I had a dream, at our old two room frame place, on the west side, the log house. Peggy and me were walking. And I seen the tree I planted across the other side of the window. The wind was blowing. I got up and I was going to peek into that other door frame. I seen carpet that was pink and beautiful. And my mother was sitting on the bed. Really beautiful bed. She was really happy to see me. She was dressed kind of white like. Her complexion is different. Just like white. And she was really happy to see me, and I wanted to go to her, but I can't. I looked this way and saw two little girls standing. One is shorter. They have a dress like Easter. But their complexion is different. And that's my dream. The next day I was so happy. That my mother is around someplace. She's that close. She's alive. Somehow in my mind one of these girls was my sister's, who lost a little girl. I really pray about it and want to know, and God gave me a dream. There is a resurrection. She is alive. That's why I'm strong on Christ and the victory he won.

Darlene Young Bear shares a dream experience she had of her husband Kenneth. He died when her children were quite young. Darlene adds more cultural background as she explains the value of crying, the importance of the giveaway, and the Lakota value of generosity. Darlene grew up in Red Scaffold and now lives in Eagle Butte. She is a Roman

Catholic lay minister and works at the Elderly Manor.

A long time ago, everybody seemed to be related to each other, so when somebody died in their family, if one is not crying, the aunties or the uncles would go and talk to them. Even after the person is buried, if the person is not crying, they go and talk to that person until they start crying. They don't say, Come on, cry now but they talk to that person and try to bring out why. Maybe there's a reason why they're not crying. That's how they keep themselves sane. Things start to developing like you feel you're all alone, because all your older relatives are gone. Pretty soon all these modern things kind of giving me a bad time, one on top of another, and you really get stressed out. I know about it. I just tell my kids, I'm gonna have to cry because if I don't, I'm gonna get sick. I let myself go and cry. At my house.

A long time ago they use to go and cry. Now the people are gonna look at you and think there's something wrong with you! Put you in the nut house! My cousin died and that made me feel bad. So when they brought him to Church, I went in there and I cried. I cried loud. Everybody thought that it shouldn't be that way, because even the priest said, Go calm her down! But my aunties and all them they started crying too. I suppose they want to but the funerals around here, they don't allow nobody to cry out like that. They will come and tell you, Don't cry, don't cry, it's all right, it'll be OK. It's not gonna be OK! But that's one of the things that happens. When they start having revivals, or prayer meetings, people will start bringing out whatever it is that is hurting them, they start crying. Now they're saying it's good when they cry.

That's the Lakota way. I don't know about the other tribes. Because my husband is a Hidatsa and he said not to cry for them all the time. Because that makes the spirit kind of hang around, don't want to leave. So he said not to cry all the time.

As a Lakota, the giveaway was a way to show that what you give, means nothing to you, but the person is more, means more to you. So you give your best. The Indian way is in appreciation to give away. But a lot of them got that white man way of thinking so that money is the only thing that's important now. If they don't have it, limited or anything, they don't want to give up anything. I always tell them that you give. Scriptures says that you give and you'll get back.

People always say, Oh, I had a dream or Oh, I saw him. People would hear about their men. And I didn't dream about him for a long time. Because he was a medicine man, I wondered what happened. I was all by myself in the house. I was going to get out, stand up and do something, but I felt bad. Why did this happen to me? So I sat down and I laid down on the couch, and I was saying my rosary and I must have went to sleep. I was laying there and I went and laid down in my dream. Here he come and he sat down and he lifted up my feet as he sat down. He was holding my legs on his lap. I looked at him and I thought, You're supposed to be dead!, I thought. He said, Don't ever think that I'm gone. I'm always gonna be with you. You'll never be alone. Another time I dreamt I was going down kind of a riding trail, no cement or pavement or anything, and trees on each side. My husband come and he grabbed hold of my hand so we was holding hands as we were going. He said, Where are you going? So I said, To the rummage sale. Here he said, You shouldn't be going to those. So I looked at him and I said, Why? He just looked straight, he was always dressed cowboy, he had a brown hat, and said, There's a lot of bad things going on now. OK, I said. After that I never go to rummage sales. I just woke up, and that day I feel happy that I saw him and he was looking good, and he wasn't having a hard time. So I was happy, that he was around to tell me things.

What they're giving away was that person preparing herself for death. So she'd start saving her things. Then they give away whatever is hers. When my husband died I gave away his stuff. That bed. He always said he was gonna give it away because it was really hard and I don't like to lay on it. I gave it away too and everybody said, Look at that! How come you give it away? That was his. Afterwards we prepare for the memorial. They said that's the toughest thing because you wear black, to be a humble person. You don't go in a crowd and argue, be loud, just be quiet.

That's the time you have to prepare for going on with your life and with the missing of that one person. It makes you more sad. When my husband died I felt like going to a pow wow. We did and when I got to the pow wow, it seems I want to look for him. To see if he's there.

Darlene's story shows how cultures can clash. The expectation of loud crying conflicts with ideal of holding up well. Giving everything away is contrary to white man's ways of holding on to possessions. Darlene found consolation, and even conversation, in the dream experiences of her husband. She declared strong opposition to the it will be OK line people so casually throw out. It is important to validate, and not dismiss, the

87

strong feelings that the death of a loved one can evoke. Pastoral ministers who come out of a culture or worldview with different expectations of dreams need to be aware of the importance people place on them. A second cultural concept to be mindful of is the Lakota view of spirits.

SPIRITS

Some people tell of actual experiences of the spirit of the deceased person during religious ceremonies. An overview of Lakota spirituality may help to understand the experience of the spirit in grieving. Lakota spirituality holds that the soul has an immortal quality. As Finger explained, Anything that has a birth must have a death. The **Wakan** (holy) has no birth and it has no death. The spirit, the ghost, and the familiar of man are not born with him but are given to him at the time of his birth. They are **wakan** and therefore will never die. (Walker, 1983, p. 9)

The Lakota view of a person's spirit or soul is multifaceted, with four aspects. When asked if the Lakota belief meant that people have multiple souls, Oglala Medicine Men involved in Christian - Lakota dialogue rejected that idea. (Stolzman) But nowhere are these Lakota traditions systematically defined. There are different opinions and descriptions about the nature of the spiritual world, but common words and concepts that are used. In conversation the English words spirit, soul and ghost are often used interchangeably. Four aspects of the soul are traditionally distinguished: (Amiotte)

- **Ni**, or **niya** is often translated as spirit, or breath. **Ni** is the source of life for the body. When a person dies their **ni** leaves them.
- **Nagi**, or **wanagi,** is the ghost like image of a person's form. **Nagi** is the element of the soul which is free from the physical constraints of the body and can leave the body during sickness, visions and dreams. **Nagi** can travel to parts of the spirit world, or other parts of the physical world to see and learn things. Good spirits and bad spirits are both **nagi**. When a person dies the **nagi** lingers close to loved ones that it longs for, usually for four days. Then it begins the journey along the Ghost path, **wanagi**

chanku,[1] and makes its way toward the Spirit World, said to be up in the stars of the Milky Way. The stars along this trail are said to be the campfires of traveling spirits.[2]

- *Sicun*, is the spirit-like power that all things possess. Everything in creation, plants, rocks and animals has *sicun*, which is immortal. *Sicun* is given by the supernaturals as a guardian spirit. When a person dies, their *sicun* returns to the supernaturals. "Because the *sicun* of things is immortal, reincarnation is possible. Sacred men are usually invested with the sicun of a deceased sacred man." (W. Powers, 1975, p. 52)

- *Taku Skan Skan*, (also *Taku kan kan*) is that which causes all life to move and live. When a baby is born, its body is animated by the spirit of movement. (DeMallie and Parks, p. 30)

It is the *nagi* that attracts the most attention, especially regarding times of death and grieving. The *nagi* is said to dwell close to the grave. During the times the Keeping of the Soul ceremony is being performed, the *nagi* is at rest. A restless *nagi* with unfinished business may wander the earth, with no home. Lakota Christians like *Doris Hump* (page 91) believe that prayers can help the restless spirits, who can no longer pray for themselves.

The *wanagi*, particularly right after death, is dangerous because it grieves for its loved ones and will try to entice its family to join it. In order to appease the *wanagi*, the parents or loved ones will "keep" it for one year. Ghost keeping is accomplished by feeding the wanagi. Sacred men can learn things from it, particularly how to

---

[1] They speak also of the '*wanagi tipi*', *house of the spirits*, and say of one who has died, '*wanagi yate iyaya*', *gone to the spirit land*. And the road over which it passes is called '*wanagi tacanku*', *spirit's path*. (Riggs, p. 213)

[2] One oral tradition tells that *Tate* (the wind), hid the entrance to the spirit trail from wandering spirits until they justified themselves by good deeds. The evil spirits remained around earth and caused suffering. (Walker, 1983, p. 373) Another oral tradition holds that at the end of the journey, at a fork in the road, spirits are met by an old woman, *maya winuhcala* (Ghost Woman, Owl Woman). She guards a cliff and judges actions and deeds. The good go to the right and are united with *Wakan Takan*. The bad or evil go to the left and are pushed over a cliff and return to earth. (Kramer p. 173) People who do not follow the Red Road, the virtuous path in life, lose their way on the journey to the spirit world and are said to wander (*onuniya u*) forever. (Short Feather, in Walker 1991, p. 115) They are pitiful and hungry. People who remember and have pity on their plight toss these spirits bits of food before each meal.

cure the sick. . . . Oglalas [Lakota] believe that the *nagi*
(ghost) of a person lingers near the place where he died
and for one year attempts to lure loved ones away. (W.
Powers, 1975 p. 131)

Because the spirits are at times considered dangerous, many Lakota people approach Lakota religious ceremonies with a degree of caution.

There are some things done in the Indian way
that I'm leery about. My dad said that if you don't
understand, stay away from that stuff. If one of
those ceremonies is done at a funeral I'm at, then I
just pray for protection. (*Doris Hump*)

How much of the traditional view of the spirit world do people on
Cheyenne River maintain? That varies from absolute acceptance, to
unfamiliarity, and includes those who totally dismiss it. A detailed exploration is beyond the scope of this project. But elements of that spirituality surface in the interviews. Chapter three reviews directions the social
sciences have to offer in working with people's experience of ghosts and
spirits. For now, here are a few brief examples of the tradition which
came out in the interviews.

The ones that die, the young ones, especially a
little one, are scared out there in the spirit world, so
they hang around with their family. People see them
or hear them because they can't go. So that's when
they have a medicine man call on another of their
dead relatives to help show the child the way,
because the little kid is scared and can't go. (*Darlene*
Young Bear)

Some say the spirits may travel to take care of
unfinished business. I've heard this described as
back sliding. World War II veterans' spirits might go
across the ocean for a while. On the forth day, the
spirit returns to the body. (*Elsie Slides Off*)

It's common to see the dead. They're telling you

they're OK and let you know not to worry, especially when you are grieving so hard. They can also give bad messages. If something's going to happen they may appear. White owls bring messages of warning. You're supposed to pray. They always say that when they die, their spirit leaves them and that spirit goes back to the place where they love to be. The spirit doesn't go anyplace away from earth. They're still here. But in those four days, if you pray for them, then their spirit is at rest. They're not going to be wandering spirits. If somebody dies and you keep seeing them, or hearing them, then their spirit is not at ease. They're lost. Or they always say, It wasn't time for them to go. So you pray for them and have ceremonies. (*Doris Hump*)

There are two kinds of owls. One is just a bird and that one always hoots three times. When it's a ghost, it will only hoot twice. Real slowly. The horse is really afraid of ghosts, and they know ghosts. (*Ted Knife*)

Grandma used to tell us not to be out alone at night, outside, especially when it's windy. They used to say ghosts were more active then. (*Peggy Knife*)

Elsie Slides Off is from Thunder Butte and is one of the very traditional elders living in the Elderly Manor in Eagle Butte. She has been called upon by area schools and organizations to help pass on cultural ways to future generations. In addition to sharing thoughts about death in a Lakota context, Elsie includes her experience of encountering her husband's spirit in a ceremony.

My cousin died. He had cancer. And I have another brother that has cancer and is suffering right now. But we have to kind of accept what is coming, from the time that they're sick until the end. For people, older people, they understand. We try to help as

91

much as we could by taking them to Indian medicine man and asking for prayers. Sometimes, if they get to a medicine man before it's too late and they get well, then we don't go suffering like this. If we get there late and the cancer spreads, there's nothing we can do about it. The spirits themselves will tell us they can no longer help them because he's too far gone.

Let me tell you about the dead person. They say they're still with them. They know and they see you. But they can't communicate. You can't see them but their spirit is there with them. And handling the body - a long time ago, they had to make their own scaffold, so they handled the body. When they lift up a dead body, your arms hurt really hurt, for some reason. So they're not supposed to really do that. I couldn't believe it until I found out myself. My little baby sister died. We brought the body back from the hospital so they brought a casket to put her in. I put some clothes on the baby and helped wrap her in a blanket. I put her in that casket. She was gonna be buried. Afterwards I couldn't use my arms for four days. They hurt me so much I couldn't even lift up. So I always believe that.

After, you have to mourn one whole year. If you don't cry, you get sick. Crying helps. You really have to cry. In that time, way back when the women folks wear black. All through that year. One year. It's not just one dress that they wear, but they have others. But they're all black. And they cut their hair. Some don't wear no hair ties or nothing. That goes on for one whole year. During that time, they have to stay home all that time. Parties, they can't go to that. The next year, the same day, you have the memorial. And that's when they take off their black clothes. They can go back to singing or dancing. But that's one year that you are really strict with it. You can't go to dances. You can't dance. They have to keep on those black clothes. I've seen it all happen.

The spirits really doctor people and one of the spirits talked to me. He said he used to live a hundred years ago and he said he died. But he said his spirit was still living to help people. So those are old medicine men that died long time ago. And his spirit don't die. They come into our ceremonies to help us.

We believe in calling in spirits during the ceremony. And you can talk to them. So I talked to my husband after he died. The spirit came in, so I talked to him. And he said, You don't have to be crying. Some of the grandchildren have no place to go, so they're going to be staying with you, he said. Stay with them and don't be crying anymore, because you're going to be sick if you do. He made me touch his hair and his face. He said, I need a haircut. He always had a short haircut. And that was him. And he talked to one of my daughters too. He told me and he left. And here after that, I never felt lonesome or nothing. And then all my grandchildren came at once after and took care of me.

They always tell us not to talk about the dead person. Never call his name. That's what they always tell us. They said don't call his name. Don't say his name. We say uncle, or how we're related to them, and that's all we say.

Elsie's tangible encounter with her husband's spirit emphasizes that the traditional Lakota worldview is vastly different from the assumptive worlds of most ministers unfamiliar with Native American Spirituality in general or the Lakota ways in particular. The encounter brought her great comfort and helped her move on and take care of her grandchildren.

A variety of practices exist regarding talking about the dead. In the traditional way, Elsie would never say their name, but would refer to them only by her relationship with them. In many of the other accounts found in this chapter, people freely use the names of their deceased relatives. People who will only indirectly talk about those who have died are not exhibiting denial, but following their cultural way of grieving.

One of the reasons Lakota do ceremonies is to put themselves in right relationship with the spirits, their relatives. The emphasis is not on the spirits relationship with God, but on their relationship with their relatives. Spirits are able to warn, help and direct. But it is important for the living to remember them and fulfill their end of the ritual. *Debbie Day* referred to having fulfilled her promise when she held Ryan's memorial and giveaway.

HABITS (*AYA*)

The Lakota believe that one's behavior during the four days following a death is critical.

> **Everything is four days. If you're grieving, you're supposed to wait. In those four days you're supposed to prepare yourself and take care of yourself, - like renew yourself. And try to be the person you want to be. A better person. In those four days, what you do is how you're gonna be for the rest of your life. That's where they say, *aya*. That's a habit. So during all those days be humble, be good, think good, while you grieve.** (*Doris Hump*)

While the goal is to keep thinking positive and getting into good habits, this four-day time span can set people up for a fall if they develop destructive habits.

> **Habits, like drinking beer. You'll be creating a negative habit for the rest of your life. You might be the worst drunk in town. You might never be able to**

94

break that habit until another death in your family. It might take your whole family [dying] before you learn to quit. (*Rev. Richard Charging Eagle*)

One reason these four days are critical is because of the Lakota belief that the spirit of the deceased is present.

During the time they said the spirits are around the home for four days, so you are not supposed to be quarreling, arguing over anything, or causing trouble, hurting somebody. For four days they have to do that, working quietly and not bothering anybody. Those are the things that stay with us after the four days is up. The old people tell us that. (*Elsie Slides Off*)

Elsie gave the example of her grandchildren. After they worked around the house for four days following a death, **they changed their ways and were very good. Now those are all still going strong like that.** Lakota people believe that habits, either good or bad, can be ingrained during this critical time. Chapter three explores some possible implications of this and other Lakota cultural beliefs about dreams and spirits, on the dynamics of grieving.

SUMMARY

This chapter has presented stories of grieving, the lived experience of a representative group of Lakota Catholics from the Cheyenne River Sioux Tribe. These stories bring to the surface several aspects of grieving that people in this community commonly face, namely, traumatic deaths, conflicted grieving, and multiple loss. These interviews also sketch a part of Lakota cultural understanding of expected behavior when death occurs, and of a worldview in which dreams, spirits and habits play a significant role.

These stories are only parts of much longer interviews. The words are directly from the pain and the wisdom of local people who have experienced loss. I have attempted to treat these stories with respect and care. The editorial decisions about what to include to give the reader a sense of life and death on Cheyenne River have been my own. I realize that as an editor or interpreter, I bring limitations and biases to the process. There are issues and insights that I will have overlooked, misrepresented, or taken for granted. That makes it crucial for the listening and dialogue to continue.

After the completion of each of these interviews, people remarked that it felt good to tell their story. They said reflecting on what they went through, with the help of some time and distance from the immediacy of the death, was therapeutic. Grieving persons not only do not mind being asked about how the death is affecting them; most long for people to ask them and openly welcome the chance to remember and share.

While Lakota culture has many resources to help people grieve, people can still get stuck. *Suzie Eagle Staff* summarized several areas that get in the way of grieving. She mentioned not crying, not having the ability to deal with the strong emotions experienced, and the use of alcohol to numb the pain as ways that can interfere with people's grieving. If people are facing a loved one's traumatic death, unresolved conflict with the one who died, or multiple loss, getting stuck will only become that much more compounded. Chapter Three picks up those themes in the exploration of the dynamics of grieving.

Chapter Three

Dynamics
of
Grieving

During my assignment as a parish priest on Cheyenne River, I regularly ministered to people in the immediate circumstances of a family member's death. I talked with them about what they might expect during their grieving. I told them that they would experience a lot of ups and downs, with conflicting and confusing emotions. I mentioned grief could creep up on them in unexpected ways and at surprising times. I warned that grief might hit them hard after all the activity surrounding the planning of the funeral was over. I tried to let them know it was OK to get angry at God or at the one who died. I told them that the feelings of grief would take time before feeling resolved.

All of those assumptions have some truth to them. But ministry to grieving people made me realize there were a lot of gaps in my understanding of grief. As I returned to school, an area I needed to explore in doing this project was what the tradition of the social sciences offers in understanding the dynamics of grieving.

GRIEF AND GRIEVING

As I mentioned in the introduction, I have learned to understand grief as the feelings that come with the loss of someone or something close to us. Grieving is what we do with those feelings. Rando (pp. 20-24) explains that grief is natural; its absence in the face of loss is abnormal. Grief is experienced in every corner of a person's life. Grief affects people psychologically, influencing moods, perceptions, attitudes and spirituality. Grief affects behavior, influencing conduct and actions. People's social worlds, their reactions and interactions with others, are impacted by grief. People physically react to grief, experiencing tightness, heightened sensitivity to noise, shortness of breath, weak and aching muscles, dry mouths, lack of energy and fatigue. Other common experiences associated with grief are:

shock	numbness	disbelief	anxiety
sadness	relief	meaninglessness	despair
loneliness	anger	confusion	guilt
yearning	apathy	crying	dreams
hallucinations	restlessness	sleep disturbance	appetite disturbances
forgetfulness	social withdrawal	substance abuse	sense of presence

searching & calling for deceased   preoccupation with person or events
reminders of the dead person (Littlewood, p. 41)

Grief is sometimes referred to as an abnormality. But loss is a norma part of every life. Death and loss can strike at any time and leave peopl feeling vulnerable and out of control. The term, complicated grief, is als used, but all grief makes life complicated. While all grief is messy and dis ruptive, it may be further complicated by the relationship to the lost pe son. There are other instances when the grief is complicated by the mar ner of death. Grief happens, but that does not need to lead to fatalism c paralysis. There are many choices about how we can grieve.

Grief does not occur in a standard way, or in an expectable, order fashion. (Littlewood, p. 16) Churchill criticizes the widespread attempt to impose Kübler-Ross's stages of dying onto the grieving proces Responding to one's own dying, and grieving someone else's death ar quite different undertakings. Assigning a stage to the emotions a perso is feeling is not especially helpful. If a person is angry, a better pastor response is to find out what they are angry about, and explore what th death means to them. Theories that focus exclusively on stages of griev ing wrongly suggest that we come to an end in our grieving as we eithe complete the stages or at last recover. In effect, they suggest that we ca somehow finish coping with mystery. (Attig, p.45) Ministers should loo beyond stages to the story of the grieving person.

Good grieving is more proactive than reactive, which requires thos grieving to choose to undertake constructive actions instead of passivel waiting for grief feelings to pass.

> The first step in coping is to resist [grief's] attractions,
> to break its hold. As we resist, we no longer perceive
> ourselves as helpless victims of choiceless death events.
> Instead, we adopt a new active posture as persons who
> can do and say at least something meaningful in the face
> of our losses. (Attig, p. 41)

Grieving can be viewed as a time of tragic opportunity which ma even lead to deep personal growth and self awareness. (Attig, p. 150)

Bereavement is an event which I was or am powerless to prevent as an event, yet the influence upon me of this event is something which I *can* affect, the bereavement as experience is something in which I can take an active, even if not dominant, role. This experience, though it hurts me, can also enhance my life. (Nute, in Bane, p. 85)

The social sciences emphasize that grieving is an activity rather than a feeling. Since grieving is what people do in response to loss, it is important to discover the tasks and activities that make for good grieving.

TASKS IN GRIEVING

Rando proposes a 6 R description of the grieving tasks necessary for survivors:

Recognize the loss. The reality of all that has been lost needs to be acknowledged. While that may seem obvious, this is precisely what many in the contemporary western world try to avoid.

React to the separation. People need to experience the feelings death stirs up inside, express those feelings, and look at the issues raised in order to begin working through the emotional turmoil.

Recollect and Reexperience the deceased and the relationship. The ability to tell stories, to begin creating memories of the deceased, is a significant grieving task. Furthermore, speaking about the deceased in the past tense helps grievers accept the reality that the deceased is truly gone. In reexperiencing, survivors can reclaim and acknowledge that much of what the deceased has given to them in relationship always remains. We lose a lot when someone dies, but we do not lose everything. We do not lose the time spent with one another, or the memories of what they taught and gave, or how they inspired and influenced. The importance of such relationships can continue even after death. (Attig, p. 171)

Relinquish the old attachments to the deceased and the old assumptive world. Psychosocial ties to the deceased must be loosened, for they cannot nurture and sustain in the same way any more. The key word is loosened and not forgotten. One of the most important aspects of grieving is finding ways to make a transition from caring about others who are

99

present to caring about them when they are absent. (Attig, p. 39)

Readjust to move adaptively into the new world without forgetting the old. Death does call for changes in patterns and routines. The absence of the one who died may necessitate learning new ways of surviving in the world without them.

Reinvest in the development of new relationships. (Rando, p. 25 Worden and Lindemann in Attig, p. 47-48)

These tasks are goals that to some degree can be successfully com pleted. But they are also ongoing life processes. Recollecting, for exam ple, obviously continues throughout a lifetime. A person might recognize a new aspect of the loss of a parent when they themselves become a par ent. These tasks place simultaneous demands on the griever. When we are grieving, we can work on several of the tasks, or focus on the most pressing one, in any order. Grievers get stuck when any of these tasks are avoided.

Lakota grieving practices help people accomplish those tasks in sev eral ways. Recognition of what is being lost is an ongoing process, but the cultural value in talking openly about death is a healthy start. Emotional reaction is encouraged by the community rather than discour aged. *Darlene Young Bear* (page 84) said that tears are expected and if you see someone not crying, you should approach them and help them to let their emotions out.

Lakota wakes provide a place to recollect and remember with story telling. During my interviews, people told stories that not only reinforced the memories, they made meaning out of what had changed for them since the deaths. If people choose to grieve by the Keeping of the Soul ceremony they talk daily with the spirit for one year. One is expected to do a review of life, to look back and relive your experiences with them (Black Bear Jr., p.4B) But there does come a time to relinquish and release the soul. The cultural practice of burning of clothes and giving away of personal possessions also fosters letting go.

Readjusting life's routines is expected and encouraged. Grieving peo ple cut back on social functions like pow wows in order to attend more to family matters. If a memorial will be held, much work is required (bead ing, sewing, carving) to make items to be given away. These gifts not only reaffirm the relationship the recipient had with the deceased, but they also solidify the connections between the living. The Wiping of Tears ceremony welcomes people back into the community and shows them how others want to offer help and support. This encourages the reinvesting in new relationships.

Persons can faithfully carry out every grieving ritual their society requires and still not work through their grief. There are other factors which may make grieving more difficult, particularly when the cause of death is traumatic, when conflict with the deceased enters the picture, and when multiple loss is involved.

ISSUES THAT COMPLICATE GRIEVING

Behaviors which point toward unresolved/unsuccessful grieving are:

- denial of the death
- denial of the painful impact of the loss
- use of a vicarious object as replacement
- prolonged unresolved grief (Engel, in Rando, p. 115)

Reacting and relinquishing were the two tasks I discovered Lakota parishioners most frequently stuck in. *Doris Hump* (page 61) recalled her dad's and brother's deaths by saying, **Now that I start talking about them it's like it just happened yesterday. I really get emotional about it. But I know that I'll never get over grieving for them.** I observed parishioners experience the feelings a death stirred up, but have difficulty getting beyond the immediacy and the intensity of the emotional reaction. That reaction often remained, even after many years.

A fixation on some point in the process, like rehashing the death scene over and over, can point to difficulty in relinquishing. People struggle with the loosening of emotional ties that relinquishing demands. For the longest time, *Peggy Knife* (page 69) could not get the moment of her brother's death out of her mind. **I just went through the motions of going back to work. I didn't talk to people. I didn't care what happened in the past, I didn't even care about the future. That moment! Hard to get through that moment.**

Another example of becoming fixated is mummification, where time becomes frozen and the deceased person's room and belongings become like a shrine that must remain unchanged. (Littlewood, p. 56) The Lakota tradition of giving away all the personal belongings of the deceased may help to avoid that problem, but that is not practiced so completely by many tribal members. *Debbie Day* (page 60) told of how she had managed to release some of her son's belongings, but that she still kept a lot, which served as a constant reminder of him. And even though physical possessions are given away, the relationship can still be frozen in time.

Unresolved grieving can be due to over-identification with the dead. This often happens when the griever can think of no other ways to keep the relationship alive. Some of us may remain in grief for fear that if they stop longing for those they have lost, they will stop loving them. (Attig, p. 39) Agents of pastoral care can work with grieving persons to find ways that keep memories alive *and* facilitate letting go. *Louis Jewett* (page 50) spoke of the importance of not forgetting, but going on with living. Mental health and pastoral care workers on Cheyenne River report the problem of many Lakota people being stuck in their grief, and this dynamic of over-identifying with the dead may explain some of the dynamic at work.

Monica Lawrence, with IHS Field Health Services, told me in an interview of the problem she calls masked grieving. Even though people go through the motions of the wake and funeral rituals, she still sees a lot of unresolved grieving. People try to act as though nothing is bothering them, but when they are using alcohol, they will cry, get sentimental about their losses, and may talk directly about what is bothering them. Later, when they are sober, they will even avoid seeing the mental health care worker again or following up on the issues raised, because those feelings are too painful to face.

Remaining in grief can bring secondary rewards, such as attention, sympathy, understanding and patience, from others. Some of us semi-consciously or unwittingly adopt a posture of permanent grieving in order to hold on to these secondary rewards. (Attig, p. 39) While that may feel good in the short term, it can block the growth that comes from working

through the grief. People may need encouragement to resist the attrac-
tions of grief and begin to address the tasks of grieving. (Attig, p. 60)

But grieving may be made more difficult by the circumstances of death
and the relationship to the one who died. Chapter two began exploring
the Lakota experience of traumatic death, conflicted grieving and multiple
loss. Lakota people frequently encounter death in a disruptive way. This
poses ongoing complications that their practices of grieving must help
them cope with.

TRAUMATIC DEATH

The general decline in infant and child mortality in the United States
has drastically changed the intensity of grief when a young person dies.

> The demographic fact of the almost certain survival
> of children born today in our country has made possible
> the development of intense and intimate ties between
> parents and children, . . . [Consequently, a young per-
> son's death causes] wounds which would be intolerable
> if the death of children were as common now as it was
> two centuries ago. (Simon Yudkin, in Toynbee, p. 47)

Due to suicide, disease, accidents and infant mortality, a staggering 15
per cent of the total population in the Aberdeen IHS Service Unit area can
be expected to die before reaching the age of twenty-four. (Appendix
Four) There is still a strong sense that it is not right when a child dies, so
these deaths evoke deep wounds. The community must face the traumatic nature of these deaths not sporadically, but over and over again.

Death of a child: The Lakota nation values children as sacred.
Wakanheja, the word for children, contains the root word **wakan**, or holy.
Babies that die before coming to full term on Cheyenne River, even if they
are tiny fetuses, are usually buried by the family rather than being dis-
posed of by the hospital. The services may be as simple as a home made
box buried on a hill near family land, or there may be a full scale funeral.
Besides just losing what they had at one time, children's deaths cause
parents to grieve for the loss of what they will never have. Debbie Day
spoke about the death of her dream of handing their ranch over to her son

Ryan to raise his own family on.

Sprang and McNeil (p. 23) observe that parents usually turn to religion to seek some meaning when a child dies. That was true of parents that worked with who faced their child's death. Whether their faith is destroyed or strengthened may depend on how successfully the religious tradition helps them in the search to make sense of the tragedy. The why question is never adequately answered. Self blame, shame and guilt are also normal parental reactions when a child dies. *Debbie Day's* grief (page 60) was compounded by people actually claiming her son's death was God's punishment for her wrongdoing. Ministers can draw upon the religious tradition to emphasize God's mercy for those burdened with guilt and God's care for those steeped in sorrow.

Absence of body for burial: Another reality in traumatic death may be the absence of a body, as in the case of *Iyonne Garreau's* (page 72, brother Blueie, who died missing in action in Korea. *Suzie Eagle Staff* (page 80) told of the difficulty cremation may also pose for Lakota people whose culture places such a high value on seeing the body and saying a personal goodbye. Grieving is made more difficult when the casket is left closed, with no chance to view the body, as is done sometimes after fires or bad accidents. Yet protecting people from the immediate shock and horror may lead to uncertainty later. The absence of a body calls for finding symbols and rituals that will help people come to terms with the reality of the loss and then express their grief.

Homicide: If the death is by homicide, ministers may be dealing with a family who has the added burdens of dealing with the police and the FBI. In an interview, *J. D. Kessling* pointed out that in South Dakota the pathologist does not work on weekends, which is when most of the traumatic deaths occur. Families must wait before being able to receive the body, for nothing can proceed until after the autopsy. Problems like these can intensify already raging emotions. Delays in the funeral can result, which may be significant if the family believes burial should take place on the fourth day.

Suicide: Some cultures have a history of honorable suicide. In times of war, when a Lakota elder could not keep up with the rest of the group

104

and put them in danger, they sometimes chose to separate themselves from the camp and wander off alone. But the suicide of a young person was never acceptable. Lakota winter counts from 1759 - 1912, record three suicides by youths. (Walker, 1982, p. 123-157) Those events made such an impact on the community that they became the defining event by which the tribe remembered the entire year.

Suicide, which has a high incidence on Cheyenne River, is an example of how the manner of death can complicate the grieving.

> The person who commits suicide puts his psychological skeleton in the survivor's emotional closet - he sentences the survivor to deal with many negative feelings and, more, to become obsessed with thoughts regarding his own actual or possible role in having precipitated the suicidal act or having failed to abort it. (Rando, p. 523)

Suicide is by no means a victimless crime. It leaves many victims in its wake. After a suicide, survivors are often denied the usual network of social supports because shame and blame are passed around more than words of consolation and sympathy. Often people must grieve alone and in silence. After his son's apparently self-inflicted gunshot wound, *Chuck LeCompte* (page 66) found out that people just seemed not to come by to visit as much, or stayed away altogether.

In the Roman Catholic church, the prohibition against suicide is so strong that at one time those who killed themselves were denied church services and burial in the church cemetery. That happened on Cheyenne River as recently as the 1970's. That practice took away the comfort the community's ritual prayer could offer a devastated family. The church still considers suicide wrong, but acknowledges how disturbances and fears that lead up to someone taking their own life diminish their responsibility. Church funeral services are no longer withheld from the grieving family, but are viewed as a means of support and healing.

On Cheyenne River, while it is tragic that suicides are as frequent as they are, friends and neighbors do attend those wakes and funerals and try to offer what support they can. Still, since suicides tend to occur in family systems already under high stress, accomplishing the grieving tasks after the suicide can be difficult.

When someone dies of a suicide, people may look elsewhere to find a scapegoat to blame and displace their anger toward. Blaming the victim is seen as somehow being disloyal to their memory. In suicides, survivors need to know that it is OK to love someone *and* be angry with them. Anger does not negate the love.

Van der Bout, de Keijser and Schut suggest that obsession with accounting for the causes and potential preventability of the death may be necessary to the well-being of the grieving person. (Littlewood, p. 69) After wishing he had not let his son leave the house, the police officer part of *Chuck LeCompte* (page 66) continued to look for anything that would suggest the death of his son was not self inflicted. In cases where a body is never found, i.e., a soldier missing in action, not knowing how, or if, the person actually died complicates the grieving, and reinforces the obsession with finding out what happened.

CONFLICTED GRIEVING

A major area of complicated mourning concerns those who mourn the death of a loved one with whom they have a markedly conflicted relationship. (Rando, p. 472) This is especially true of ambivalent relationships that result from the victimization of physical or sexual abuse. For people who have been victimized, it is helpful to stress that grieving the death of an abuser does not invalidate the abuse. All ties, both positive or negative ones, need to be mourned. Indeed, often the negative ties are the ones that bind the strongest. (Attig p. 81) People may need to be reconciled and encouraged to work through their hurt and rage before they can begin to grieve. (Anderson, 1993 p. 383) Abused people can be helped by grieving what the abuser has taken away and being reminded that a prime reason for grieving is to free oneself from the bondage caused from past hurts.

One of the past hurts which surfaces on Cheyenne River is the experience of feeling abandoned. When parents are having alcohol problems it is common for their children to be placed in the care of other relatives sent away to boarding schools, or placed in group homes. For someone burdened with unresolved abandonment issues, the death of someone close will reopen those wounds.

Another reason for conflicted grieving came in an interview with *Yvon Sheehy SCJ* and *Jim Walters SCJ*, who raised the issue of survivor guilt. They gave the example of a father, driving while drunk, who ran off the road and wrecked his car. He survived, but his child died. Besides grieving the loss of his child, he now must live with the guilt of knowing he was responsible for the death. In an interview, *Gary Lantz SCJ* said that people look shamefully at the drinking, drugs, or deterioration of health happening in their family. They feel guilty because they allowed it to happen and they wonder if they could have done something to prevent the tragedy from occurring. Deaths due to such neglect can prompt shame and guilt added to the grief.

Addictions like alcoholism are the focus of dual concern. Addictions can be indicators of unresolved grieving. Addictions can also get in the way of any successful resolution. *Suzie Eagle Staff* (page 81) highlighted how for many people drinking numbs the pain, but also halts the process and hard work that grieving calls for.

Rev. Richard Charging Eagle, who worked with the tribe's alcoholism program, holds that:

> **Grieving is the number one problem for every Indian on the street. But nobody ever asked them. Finally, I asked [one man] what is it that really makes you drink? He said, The quietness and the stillness of my house. When my wife was alive, there's always children around, noises that they make. It's empty in my room and the house is so quiet. I can't handle it. We try to medicate them, but we never ask them what's really bothering you? [They have] shame because they're drinking and they do shameful things. They drink and try to forget. But all of this starts from the grieving.**

Abuse from alcoholic family situations on Cheyenne River is well known and often cited. But for cases of sexual abuse, with its devastat ing effects, there are no reliable statistics or documentation. Works like Abrogast's <u>Wounded Warriors</u> show that survivors are beginning to break the silence. The community is now becoming awakened to the wide spread tragedy that sexual abuse has been. Abuse can destroy people's self-esteem and interfere with the establishment of healthy new relation ships. An abuser's death can leave the survivor with so many mixed feel ings and reignite issues long suppressed or forgotten. In addition, the survivor may have to listen to well-meaning people, who try to comfor them by telling them what a good person their abuser was. Anger at an abuser eventually needs to be expressed and worked through in order for healing to take place.

Denial often accompanies conflicted relationships. Denial is a norma response to loss and a healthy initial coping mechanism. People may need to temporarily deny the impact of death or other trauma in order to make funeral preparations, or to give themselves a period of psychologi cal distance where internal grieving work can begin. Denial becomes problematic when people cling to it and do not address what has caused their hurts.

A strength of the Lakota way of grieving is that it steers people into constructive activities and keeps them focused on good thoughts about the deceased. Rosenblatt (p. 33) holds that keeping busy with funeral preparations may promote responses inconsistent with the expression of anger and aggression. A potential weakness however is when feelings of anger at the deceased exist and there is no model for resolving them. Brokenleg and Middleton (p. 105) claim, The Lakota grief model differs from current Western models, because denial and anger are minimal. Lakota models of denial and anger also differ from western models. But in the stories from chapter two, Lakota parishioners acknowledge many experiences of denial and feelings of anger.

MULTIPLE LOSS

Death can bring the accumulated effects of all the losses in life into the grieving process. New losses trigger memories and raise unresolved roblems caused by earlier losses. Besides *Iyonne Garreau's* experience ,ages 71-75), several of the other stories fit into this category. *Doris* *lump's* three closest friends from childhood all died in car accidents at a oung age. Any car accident causes those hard to handle feelings and 1emories to come flooding back for her. Although years had passed, the eath of Tater and Marty Ward's father brought back painful memories of 1eir mother's death. *Rosie Roach Avery* (page 76) is another who suf- 1red multiple loss; she lost two brothers in the prime of their youth.

What makes traumatic deaths particularly difficult for the Lakota peo- 1e on Cheyenne River is their multiple nature. Both the personal histo- es and the available mortality statistics (See Appendices) show that peo- le on Cheyenne River grieve multiple losses in short time spans. These an have a cumulative effect.

In addition to the biological deaths, *Rosie Roach Avery* (page 77))uched on the losses of culture, language and land that are a part of akota reality. Those can contribute to a sense of multiple loss. *Austin* .*eith* argues that Lakota people commonly suffer the same psychological ffects as prisoners of war do in Post Traumatic Stress Syndrome ecause of all these losses and trauma. (Native American Development :enter)

In cultures like the Lakota, where people experience family *tiyospaye*) in a broad sense, death strikes the family more often that it ,ould when the family is only a nuclear unit. When an aunt who is con- idered a mother to her nieces and nephew dies, it may evoke the same ind of intense feelings of loss as when a biological parent dies. 'urthermore, family ties are not limited to blood. The Lakota have a mak- 1g-a-relative ceremony, called **hunkayapi**, which establishes a relation- hip that is the same as blood kinship. Even if people are not made rel- tives formally, there are always informal family ties. *Doris Hump* (pages ,2-63) mentioned how the family friend who lived with them was treated s a grandfather. *Rosie Roach Avery* (page 77) added, **With grief you** **eally have to look at not necessarily just the family unit, you have** **o look at the extended family unit . . . it reaches out into the com-** **nunity, because there's more relatives, and it gets even bigger,**

across the reservation. With any death, ministers need to be aware c
the possibility of this far reaching impact.

Grieving is not done by isolated individuals, but by people-in-relation
ship, people who are part of the social network of the *tiyospaye*.
Studies of grief processes in both the psychological
and pastoral literature have focused on the person as a
self-contained unit and have tended to ignore the larger
ramifications of 'grief work' in family life . . . Family and
marital relationships, because of their intensity and significance, offer a primary arena for working out one's feelings regarding recent or old losses. (Richard Bruehl, in
Bane p. 92-93)
Relationships with those who have died are still a real and ongoin
part of any group's dynamics, particularly so with Lakota families. Famil
systems theories raise awareness that any death within such a systen
will upset the group equilibrium and force the survivors to take on th
roles and duties, both positive and negative, that the deceased performe
for the group. Grieving within a family system includes sharing the expe
rience of the loss with each other, developing open communication, an
firming up remaining ties. Completion of these tasks allows the family t
reorganize and reinvest in new relationships and life pursuits. (Walsh &
McGoldrick, p.11)

Lakota persons face complications in grieving due to all these disrup
tive confrontations with death. They face the grieving from the perspec
tive of their own worldview and culture. In the next section we will see hov
their social context of dreams, spirits and habits affect their ways of griev
ing.

THE CULTURAL CONTEXT OF DEATH
DREAMS AND SPIRITS

Rosenblatt, Walsh and Jackson studied cross-cultural issues of grie
by looking at seventy-eight diverse cultures from around the globe. The
found that ghost beliefs and cognitions were fundamentally human fo
grieving persons. People consistently experienced stimuli that could only

be explained as an encounter with the deceased. What the cross-cultural literature seems to indicate is that belief in ghosts is natural; it is consistent with human nature. (Rosenblatt, p. 53)

American culture values rationality and logic. It generally dismisses reports of spirits or ghosts. But with all the purported emphasis on science in the contemporary western world, the degree of interest in ghosts and after death experiences is amazingly high. Business is booming at the psychic hotline. Books like Betty Eadie's Embraced By The Light, describing vivid and colorful near death experiences, have been national best sellers. Television shows ranging from Touched By An Angel to The X-Files tap into the enormous interest people have for the supernatural world. Spirits and ghosts are still very much a part of the worldview in the United States. The helping professions are learning to work with people who experience spirits rather than dismissing them.

American and European attitude toward ghost beliefs and cognitions creates problems for bereaved persons. To admit to having a conversation with a deceased person or to having seen a supposedly buried person sitting in one's living room is very risky in American society . . . If professionals who work with bereaved persons were alerted to the likelihood of ghost cognitions, they might be in a position to reduce distress in many bereaved persons and once they had shown that they were accepting of such 'deviant' mental processes, to learn much more from bereaved persons about thought processes during bereavement. (Rosenblatt, p. 57 - 58)

Persons who have ghost or spirit experiences in contemporary western culture will probably question their own sanity. Rather than talking about what happened, they often conclude that the safest action is to keep the experience to themselves. (Dombeck p. 45) When people keep silent about what has happened, the chance to work with some rich material is lost. Rosenblatt (p. 53) explains, interaction with a ghost could conceivably serve various ego needs. For example one could transact unfinished emotional, relational, or decision-making business with the deceased.

Ministry on Cheyenne River demanded that I work with grieving people around the issue of ghosts and spirits. Frequently I was called to do a home blessing when someone saw or heard a *nagi*. Grieving people sometimes stopped by the office for pastoral counseling and would talk about what they had dreamed or seen or heard. I distinctly remember the first person who came into the office and began reporting what her mother had told her the night before - and I knew the mother had been dead for several months. Part of me thought the woman was crazy, but I suspended judgment, took very seriously what she had to say and began working with her on some changes she wanted to begin making in her life because of the encounter. As time went on, I heard others talk about similar experiences. Lakota people who participate in traditional Lakota religious ceremonies commonly related to me some of their experiences with spirits. During my time of ministry on Cheyenne River, I personally had no direct encounters with spirits or ghosts. But my attitude about that reality changed over the years. Initially I was very skeptical. But I encountered a consistency in people's experience that was impossible to ignore. I began to trust and accept their reality. Just because something is outside of my experience does not mean it is not real.

The Lakota say that ghosts cannot be felt, but are seen and heard. They are frequently helpful or come to give a message. Ghosts usually appear in connection with an unwillingness to leave this world. Ghosts may signal unfinished business for the one grieving. **Some of them grieve so hard that the deceased appear to them in some way.** (*Doris Hump*)

I worked by assuming that dreams or visions of someone who died were a signal of unfinished business and I tried to explore that with the griever. One might ask, What does this mean to you? What do you think you need to do? Dreams and experiences of spirits, either in a vision or through a ceremony, can be an asset in helping Lakota people focus on unfinished grieving tasks. For *Elsie Slides Off* (page 93), the encounter with her husband helped ease her worries and led her to reinvest more in relationships with her grandchildren. For *Chuck LeCompte* (page 67) a

112

dream gave him the opportunity to give his son a hug that told of his love.

Roman Catholic tradition upholds the reality of the relationship between the living and the dead.

> Though separated from the living, the dead are still at one with the community of believers on earth and benefit from their prayers and intercession. . . The community acknowledges the reality of separation and commends the deceased to God. In this way it recognizes the spiritual bond that still exists between the living and the dead. (ICEL 1989, #6)

Even the idea that spirits hang around earth before making their final journey toward God is not foreign to the Judeo-Christian tradition. One of the reasons it made sense for Mary Magdalene to visit Jesus' tomb on the third day was because of the belief in Palestine that for three days the spirit of the dead person hovered round the tomb. (Barclay, p. 265) More theological discussion regarding Christian and Lakota understandings of spirits will prove fruitful.

HABITS (*Aya*)

Lakota belief says that habits, both good and bad, are formed during the crucial first four days of grieving. Loss makes people vulnerable and more susceptible to influences which change their thoughts and behaviors. This makes it important for people to behave respectfully and get along with others. Times of grieving can also be times of opportunity. Death is a natural time for survivors to evaluate their own life and sometimes begin the path toward significant life changes. People may even discover positive benefits from major loss. (Rando, p. 42) Awareness of death can help one view time as limited and precious, which in turn can produce an increased valuing of relationships and a heightened capacity for intimacy and empathy. (Walsh & McGoldrick, p.26) Another opportunity for growth during times of grief, is to learn to feel without avoiding the deep sorrow of irreplaceable loss, to integrate our experiences with persons we lose into our autonomous lives, and to be fully alive until we die. (Bane, p. viii).

If grieving people are able to make positive changes in the four days after death, this cultural dynamic of habits can bolster their ability to maintain those good ways. But the dynamics of habits can cause problems in grieving as well. Anger is a legitimate emotional reaction. For some people venting anger and rebelling in the face of death may be the most healthy thing they can to. To tell someone, if you act out with anger, you will be like this for the rest of your life, obviously discourages such behavior.

Rev. Richard Charging Eagle (page 94) said a person who drinks will develop an addiction and may not get the opportunity to change until someone else in their family dies. A Lakota person who copes with the stress surrounding death by drinking may feel doomed to perpetuate that self destructive habit. Belief that an unchangeable habit has formed makes them feel powerless to change. Yet one of the very purposes of ritual grieving activity is to facilitate the necessary changes the survivors need to make in light of the changing world caused by the death.

THE ROLE OF RITUAL ACTIVITY IN GRIEVING

Ritual activity can help people accept the finality of death and help them enter into grieving tasks.

> Throughout history and in every culture, mourning rituals have facilitated not only the integration of death but also the transformations of survivors . . . [The main task is to] acknowledge both the finality of death and the continuity of life. (Walsh & McGoldrick, p.1)

The power of ritual lies in giving people prescribed channels of action so they do not have to fall passive victim to the numbness or powerlessness they may feel. For grievers, knowing that upcoming rituals will require them to say their goodbyes and bring some closure to death may help prompt them into doing the necessary psychological work and attend to the grieving tasks. (Rosenblatt, p.8) For *Peggy Knife* (page 70) it was the giveaway and the memorial dinner a year after her brother's death that revived her from the numbness.

Ritual can allow the expression of many different realities simultaneously, such as both the pain and suffering of human loss in the face of death . . . and the theological assertion of hope and promise. (Smith, p. 3) The repetitive nature of ritual reminds those grieving not just once, but over and over, of the deceased and of their loss, but also of the hope, so that gradually all those realities can begin to sink in. (Rando, p. 313-318) Perhaps the most repetitive act I observed in Lakota grieving practices was the simple act of shaking hands and offering a few words to the survivors. This action reinforced the reality of the death, while offering the support of the community. A handshake acknowledges death's broken connection, while reaffirming life's ongoing connections. On the day of a funeral, handshakes were offered at least three times: after viewing the body; before leaving the cemetery; and after the meal and giveaway.

While completeness may be a desired goal, ritual is usually just part of the healing process. For many people, the most the funeral can do is to get them out of the initial state of shock, numbness, and denial, and into grief, that is, to help them into rather than through or out of grief. (Ramshaw, p. 71) *Peggy Knife* (page 69) reported feeling numb and in shock throughout the funeral. *Tater Ward* (page 56) commented that **the grieving really starts when the funeral is all over with.**

Ritual allows people to symbolize what family members incorporate with them from the lost person, and to symbolize how they are moving on with life. (Walsh and McGoldrick, p. 57) In symbolizing what is carried on from the lost one, grieving rituals usually contain symbols of the deceased.

> The way one treats a symbol is analogous to the way in which one would treat what it symbolizes. The symbol is inseparably entwined with the feelings and thoughts fostered about the person or event symbolized, evoking new experiences and at the same time giving form to them. (Rando, p. 323)

It is thought to be more helpful to symbolically give such items away, rather than destroying them. The Lakota rituals of giving away possessions and burning clothes and very personal items foster many thoughts and memories of the deceased person, while also reinforcing the reality that they are gone. *Louis Jewett* (page 50) described how burning his wife's clothes had greater symbolic weight than if he had simply packed them up and taken them to a used clothing store: **not getting rid of it, but the clothes went like she did, going up in the air.**

Grieving rituals bring people in contact not only with death, but with each other. Such rituals can offer a place for shared suffering within a supportive community. (Walsh & McGoldrick, p. 9)

> Liturgy enters the picture as mediator between the grief of the individual and the ability of the community to absorb that grief and transform it to hope within the community's ongoing trust in, and reliance on, the promises of the God who has spoken in its midst. (Boadt, p. 23)

Rituals such as funerals provide a special time out of time, that is, an encapsulated time frame which offers an opportunity for experiencing the overwhelming emotions that death evokes, while also containing such expression. (Walsh & McGoldrick, p. 56) Time outside of time is an apt description of Lakota ritual, where the clock is of little concern. What needs to happen unfolds in its own time and way. The entire ritual of death and burial is an interconnected whole that everyone can take part in.

Experiencing and expressing the feelings grief evokes is an important grieving task. Rituals can offer a safe place to do that because they have boundaries of both time and space. People know they have an ending and they have some idea of what to expect when they enter into a ritual. (Imber-Black, in Walsh & McGoldrick, p.207) Ritual also can be powerful because actions, the tender placing of a flower on the grave, the violent sobbing as the casket is closed for the last time, give people a way to express themselves beyond the power of words alone.

ROMAN CATHOLIC FUNERAL RITUAL

As a Roman Catholic parish priest, I had a role and a responsibility to work with grievers so the funeral services and public rituals of grieving accomplished the goals of helping people acknowledge the reality of the loss, and to begin moving them toward the life changes they needed to make in light of that loss. Rituals serve advantageously in furthering those goals. However, in order to be effective, ritual must be done well. Poor ritual sets the process back. Rituals can unfortunately be used in a way that safely distances people from the reality of death, if those assembled become spectators rather than participants. The goal of full, conscious and active participation in public worship is, however, often voiced in Roman Catholic circles. (*Sacrosanctum Concilium*, #14, in Flannery, 1975). Participants' awareness about the rituals can increase the usefulness. Rituals like funerals are more effective when they are designed or chosen with the particular needs and situations of specific grievers in mind, and when they involve not just peoples' minds, but their emotions and senses as well.

The Roman Catholic tradition of ministry to the grieving that I operate out of is molded and shaped by the <u>Order of Christian Funerals</u> (OCF)[1]. OCF views the death, wake, funeral and burial rites as parts of one interconnected whole.

> The funeral liturgy does not stand alone. Rather it participates in the much larger context of pastoral care that accompanies the events of sickness and death in our community. This includes the pastoral care of the bereaved . . . an invitation to bring our faith to bear upon the harsh realities of death and bereavement. (Rutherford, p. 9)

The invitation to look at the larger context of pastoral care reflects a shift in the focus of the funeral rites from the dead to the needs of the grieving assembly. At one time the mass for the dead primarily emphasized sending departed souls on their way to God. The rites still contain prayer and intercession for the dead, but OCF identifies the survivors who are grieving as the focus of ministerial activity.

> The church intercedes on behalf of the deceased because of its confident belief that death is not the end nor does it break the bonds forged in life. The Church also ministers to the sorrowing and consoles them in the

---

[1]International Committee for English in the Liturgy 1989, hereafter referred to simply as OCF.

funeral rites with the comforting word of God and the sacrament of the eucharist. (OCF, #4)

People often experience bewilderment and shock at death. The ministry of the church at that time is described as one of gently accompanying those grieving. (OCF #52) The rites offer support as grievers begin to adjust to the death, express their sorrow and find the hope their faith offers

While grief experiences may have common threads, each person's grief is unique, especially since each person's relationship with the deceased is unique. OCF acknowledges this diversity by offering a wider selection of prayer texts than previous editions. OCF provides prayers to be used with those grieving after the death has occurred and when people first gather in the presence of the body. Such moments can benefit from ritual prayer. Included are prayers to be used when a child dies when someone dies after a long illness, when the death is by suicide when a married couple dies. The diverse prayer selection aims a addressing the varying needs of the assembly.

The church calls each member of Christ's Body - priest, deacon, layperson - to participate in the ministry of consolation: to care for the dying, to pray for the dead, to comfort those who mourn. (OCF, #8)

OCF legitimates grieving in encouraging the bereaved to bring their grief to, and express their grief amid a supportive community of faith which will share their suffering and console. (Smith, p. 51) Increasingly in the urbanized contemporary western world, there is a tendency to pare funeral ceremonies to the bare minimum, to cause the least inconvenience to survivors and the community. Friends may briefly stop by at the house or for the wake, but only immediate family takes off work to go to a funeral. But OCF reaffirms and encourages the ministry of the assembly. When it comes time for a funeral, people often debate whether they are close enough to the deceased or to the family to justify making the effort to attend. They worry about what to say, or whether their presence will do any good, and they find an excuse not to go. The primary way the community fulfills their ministry of consolation is by actively participating in the funeral rites (OCF #11). People who doubt, or find themselves busy with other things, should be encouraged to make the extra effort and support grievers by attending, because there is great power in that kind of support. *Debbie Day* (page 59) for instance, reported what gratitude she felt at the outpouring of support in the numbers that turned out for her son's funeral. Concerned members of the community can minister to grieving families by helping with the routine tasks of daily living, which frees the family to plan and take care of the funeral rites. (OCF, #10) The neighbor who drops off a casserole for lunch, or who volunteers to make sure the horses are fed and watered, can provide a valuable service to the family busy with all the preparations. That is the kind of ministry many Lakota people model well. *Rosie Roach Avery* counsels, **If somebody close died and I heard about it right now, I'd be there for them; I'd just go.**

Another form of participation encouraged is in the planning and working through of the funeral rites. (OCF, #17) There may be some liturgical and ritual tasks that are too emotionally draining and difficult for the survivors. But since rituals can help express the grief and the hope and bring people into contact with the reality of the death, the goal is that active involvement in ritual, in as much as people are able, will help facilitate their grieving. Even children should not be overlooked. When a child dies, classmates with the appropriate abilities should be asked to serve, read, or sing. Participation is an aid to their grieving. (OCF # 242) Wakes and funerals always call for extra people to pass out booklets or move chairs around. Most people, young and old alike, are glad to be asked to help. *Rosie Roach Avery* (page 24) recalls that in the Lakota way, it is important to include children in all of the tasks possible.

Perhaps the best way to describe the pastoral richness of the OCF is to think of it as a resource book. It is in light of this normative collection of rites that each funeral will be individually shaped by the parish community . . . Once parish ministers are familiar with the OCF, they will begin with the pastoral circumstances surrounding the death. Only after that will they turn to the book for rites that best expresses the Christian meaning of death in those circumstances. As a resource book the OCF does not contain all the answers to our ritual needs. Nor does it always contain the most appropriate gestures or even all the perfect prayers. It does provide us with a normative model for expressing our faith in the midst of death's mystery. (Rutherford, pp. 18-19)

Rutherford indicates the importance of starting with the pastoral circumstances of the death. OCF serves as a resource which offers people in grief options about ritualizing their grieving. Further changes of those rituals in response to Lakota culture calls for an examination of contextualization.

CONTEXTUALIZATION OF THE ORDER OF CHRISTIAN FUNERALS

Contextualization is the process of individually shaping a normative collection of rites in response to the needs of the local community. Planning a funeral or memorial service with Lakota parishioners is always an exercise in contextualization because of the need to be faithful to Roman Catholic liturgical guidelines and to be respectful of Lakota culture. The Lakota have expected and established customs of greeting the body and saying farewells, which are two examples where contextualization within the funeral ritual would be especially helpful. The Lakota Inculturation Task Force has been formed in the Diocese of Rapid City, South Dakota, to forward the project of developing authentic Lakota Catholic worship. They see liturgical inculturation as a desirable goal.

There is no objection from the elders or the Lakota people for the use of religious symbols which are already being used — sweet grass or sage smudging, shawl, star quilt, vessels with native symbols, medicine wheel, utensils, colors, vestments with native design, Indian hymns. (Hatcher, Minutes of Lakota Integration Task Force, October 1994)

The task force cautions, however, that it is not up to outsiders to decide which Lakota symbols and rituals are appropriate for use in worship. The Lakota people themselves must make the decisions about what is appropriate, and the times and places when it is appropriate. They recommend

120

that only Lakota people lead Lakota ceremonies, which makes it more crucial to develop a partnership with traditional Lakota Spiritual leaders. Collaboration with traditional Lakota spiritual leaders raises many questions about how to structure the services. When consulting with the family to choose rites and texts that are appropriate, OCF (#16) instructs ministers to take into account the person who died, the circumstances of their death and the spiritual and psychological needs of the family and friends of the deceased. Customs of the local Christian community are to be taken into account (OCF #43). Care must be taken that the choice and use of signs and symbols are in accord with the culture of the people (OCF, #21). The importance of taking the context into account is clear.

Trying to be sensitive to people's culture, Roman Catholic liturgical books frequently use the word adaptation. Adaptation of the rituals is not just allowed or tolerated, but prescribed. When ritually gathering in the presence of the body, because cultural attitudes and practices on such occasions may vary, the minister *should* [emphasis mine] adapt the rite. (OCF, #109) The committal rite, if pastoral need dictates, is also open for adaptation (OCF, #211). Adaptations of the vigil will often be suggested by the place in which the celebration occurs. (OCF, #55) Guidelines for adaptation within the funeral mass are not found in OCF, but in the *General Instruction of the Roman Missal*. (CDW 1975) Pastoral effectiveness is said to be heightened by readings, prayers and songs that meet the needs and religious dispositions of the participants. (GIRM #313) But the church approaches any contextualization cautiously, as it safeguards things old - the deposit of tradition, while it examines and prudently brings forth things new. (GIRM 15) The dual goals of safeguarding the deposit of tradition and bringing forth new traditions are the great challenges of contextualization.

Adaptation language is problematic when it is used to imply a superficial borrowing of cultural symbols. Contextualized Lakota Christian ritual demands the introduction of Lakota culture into the life of the church (page 13). The first missionaries among the Lakota translated Christian hymns into the Lakota language, while retaining European concepts and melodies. A contextualized Christian Lakota song would most likely follow the composition and melody of an honor song, with short but meaningful repetitions, accompanied with the drum rather than the organ.

OCF mentions the importance of music as integral to the funeral rites because music, like ritual, can give expression to feelings that words alone cannot. Song texts should express the paschal mystery of the Lord's suffering, death, and triumph over death and should be related to the readings from Scripture (OCF, #30). Music can serve the goals of comforting the grievers and creating a bond among the gathered assembly. The use of honor songs (page 34) certainly express the feelings of the grievers, but they do not explicitly express the Scriptural themes nor the paschal mystery.

The use of color at funerals provides another example of a contextualization issue. The liturgical color chosen for funerals should express Christian hope but should not be offensive to human grief or sorrow (OCF, #39) Currently in the United States, white, violet and black are the colors deemed appropriate. How can a color be either appropriate for a funeral or offensive to human grief or sorrow except within a particular cultural context? There can be no such a thing as an authentic Christian color because the color of hope depends on how hope is represented in the particular Christian's cultural context. For the Lakota, red is the traditional sacred color. Lakota people who died have been traditionally wrapped in red blankets. Red is symbolic of sacrifice, especially for those who have offered their sufferings so that the people might live. Red should be considered an appropriate Christian color in the context of Lakota funeral.

The use of symbols in general raises tensions in the funeral liturgy OCF #38 questions incorporating life symbols, rather than religious symbols, into the funeral rite.

There is the tendency however, to want to place symbols of a person's life on the coffin alongside or even instead of the Christian symbols. There is obviously a human need to ensure that the life of the deceased is acknowledged and remembered in a public way in our funeral rites, but it seems that we are not quite sure yet how and where to incorporate these symbols into a rite which has an underlying baptismal theology. (Smith, p. 110)

With the mix of Lakota, cowboy and veterans traditions heavily influencing the funeral rituals on Cheyenne River, symbols as diverse as star quilts, boots and saddles, guns and the American flag, may have prominence during some part of the ceremonies. Exactly when and under what circumstances these symbols are appropriate needs to be part of an ongoing discussion.

Contextualization is necessary because no ritual, no matter how well structured, can take into account all the circumstances of the death, the survivors' relationship with the deceased, and the cultural expectations of the local community. At times Lakota and Roman Catholic rituals remain side by side, in a dimorphic dance. Contextualization, or in Roman Catholic terms inculturation, demands more integration.

CHRISTIAN SCRIPTURES AND GRIEVING

Years ago a common criticism of Roman Catholic presentation of the scriptures was that it focused too much on hellfire and brimstone and played upon people's fear. Today, the criticism comes full circle, claiming that too much focus is given to the resurrection without allowing people time and space to fully experience the cross inherent to the grieving experience. In reviewing the selection of scripture texts that are suggested for liturgical prayer throughout the events of dying and burial, the tradition is not so one dimensional in either direction, but broad and rich enough to touch people in their varied needs.

In Judaism, people in grief traditionally pray from Biblical books like Job and Lamentations during the Shiva, or seven days after burial. While death eats at one's relationship with God, as the mourner returns to life again his relationship with the God of life and death must also be renewed. (Steven Moss, in Bane, p. 113) Persons with a relationship with God can scream at God in anger and pain. Smith (p. 18) asserts, it is in these psalms of lament that we find a whole tradition which gives us permission to give vent to the full range of human emotions which arise out of loss. Boadt (p. 24) calls the psalms of lament a school of prayer in

123

which we must face life head on and not deny its difficulties, but let go of our fear to look beyond ourselves to a generous God. In the Hebrew scriptures, death is a natural part of life. No individual expected immortality, for that belongs to God alone. What was more important was the survival of the community as a people. (Ninian Smart, in Toynbee, p. 116 ff.) Bruggemann (p. 123) explains that communal grief on the part of Israel was not resignation. Israel complains, accuses, cajoles, urges, in order to get things changed. But . . . engages in no denial of loss nor any self - deception about the hurt. She faces loss and hurt fully and addresses them frontally. Because Israel addresses its grief to God, there is a chance for some answer or at least the beginning of healing.

Senior (p. 45) looks at the scripture selections chosen for Roman Catholic funeral ritual and pulls out several different themes, including God's fidelity in the midst of pain and sorrow; legitimate grief expressed in hope and faith; the value of our prayer for the dead; and the paschal mystery of suffering. Commenting on Lamentations 3: 17-26, Senior writes, a refreshing quality of many Old Testament writings is their frank expression of grief and pain. Prayer need not be diplomatic and refined. The believer felt free to express his feelings and anxieties before his God (Senior p. 45) Phrases from this passage such as I have forgotten what happiness is, my future is lost, homeless poverty, wormwood and gall and leaves my soul downcast within me, are feelings many grievers may identify with.

Psalm 63 speaks of the feelings of dryness and weariness, while longing for God. The conflicting emotions of hope in God coexist with the despair and sadness grief can bring. Senior cites Job 19: 23-27 as a passage which shows one able to face the reality of suffering and death while still maintaining hope in God.

1 Thess 4: 13-18 emphasizes the need to console one another and help each other in bearing grief with hope. Rev 21: 1-7 describes the hopes for the new heavens and new earth where there will be no more tears, mourning, crying or pain.

My point here is not to attempt a summary of everything the scriptures say about dying and grieving. Instead I hope to show how rich the tradi-

124

ion really is. The emphasis which comes forth from the tradition depends upon which texts are chosen and what the homilist draws forth from them. Sugar coating death and skipping ahead to the resurrection without experiencing the pain which loss brings is not a part of the scriptural tradition. If the pastoral need for the occasion is to focus on the grief and the feelings of anger, confusion, loneliness and despair which people may be feeling, the scriptures provide ample resources. The problem is more the contemporary attitude that shies away from that direct confrontation with death. In using the text from Matthew 11 for funerals, Come to me, all you who labor and are burdened, and I will give you rest, is the focus more commonly on the rest rather than the burden? Why not highlight both? One legitimate criticism of OCF's scripture selections is that it provides too few texts about the meaninglessness of death (Boadt, p. 25), but Boadt does not suggest which texts he would find helpful in that area.

When it comes to preaching the Christian message at funerals,

> The aim of the funeral homily is to proclaim the mystery of God's love for us in Jesus Christ, as this is attested to in the liturgical texts and also in the life of the deceased. To accomplish this the homily is shaped by a dialectic between stories from the Bible and stories about the individual being buried . . . Through the interplay of these two sets of stories God is praised, the deceased is shown respect, and the congregation is drawn more deeply into the paschal mystery. (Kreig, pp. 232, 239)

Mitchell and Anderson (pp. 153-159) have two goals to keep in mind when preaching to a grieving congregation. First of all, the preaching should openly and honestly acknowledge the loss, rather than dancing around it. Secondly, the preaching should draw upon the biblical tradition that grief is known to all God's people. This should help people claim their own uncomfortable feelings about grief, avoid a false optimism, and take courage and hope because their sufferings are shared. OCF (#141) also suggests the homily should both console and give mourners the strength to face the death with hope.

Attentive to the grief of those present, the homilist

should dwell on God's compassionate love, and on the paschal mystery of the Lord . . . also should help the members of the assembly to understand that the mystery of God's love and the mystery of Jesus' victorious death and resurrection were present in the life and death of the deceased and that these mysteries are active in their own lives as well. (OCF, #27)

OCF (#27) instructs that the funeral homily should be grounded in the scriptural readings chosen for the occasion and warns against turning the preaching event into a eulogy. The prohibition against eulogies is not aimed at stopping personal reference, but at a style of formal address that omits the gospel message and replaces it with a focus on the achievements of the deceased. If there is to be some words of remembrance they should come at the end of mass and not be longer than the homily lest it skew the sense of proportion. (Smolarski, 1997)

The warning about not eulogizing is so that the preaching does not become a speech praising someone's accomplishments, but connects God's word to the immediate situation of life and death and addresses those who are grieving. This does not mean the homily should be impersonal or avoid any mention of the deceased. On the contrary, personal anecdotes will not sidetrack the homily: tastefully and thoughtfully done they can effectively illustrate the scripture message. (Senior, p. 38) People appreciate and remember the personal touches, which can help them appropriate the gospel message. *Tater Ward* said that the homily at his dad's funeral worked because it was directed,

Towards church, and also toward the kind of life that dad led. It talked about his background. Putting it into words sure helped. Some funerals you go to the homily is more about church, and not the one who died. You shouldn't forget about the person that's dead.

Awareness of Lakota culture adds another dimension to the preaching task. Religious leaders who speak to and for the community are expected to reaffirm and uphold the moral values of the community.

If the death is a result of negligence, the speaker will first acknowledge the state of grief that the community, and especially the family, is experiencing. Then a most stern and direct reprimand will be given publicly to those who have acted negligently; this is endured and accepted without question. The speaker will address the people compassionately and urge them to make some resolution as a future preventative measure. (Brokenleg and Middleton, p. 109)

Death is an occasion that makes people pause and evaluate how they have been living and to take responsibility for their actions. When I first heard Lakota preachers speak critically and forcefully to a grieving family, my sensibilities, filled with God-is-love imagery, were offended. I harshly judged that they were doing more harm than good. But this type of preaching is also prophetic. In Lakota culture, the four-day period after death is a crucial time to make necessary and lasting changes. Warnings and admonitions reinforce that value. I had to reexamine my perspective and appreciate what Lakota preachers were attempting to do for the congregation. Dialogue about what messages the community needs to hear will lead to a greater cross-cultural understanding.

MISCONCEPTIONS ABOUT GRIEVING

Rando identifies several misconceptions[2] we commonly have about grieving. These misconceptions provide a framework for summarizing and identifying areas needing further exploration. Faulty assumptions about grieving can lead people away from the kinds of actions they need to be working on, which can complicate grieving. The personal histories in chapter two show how these false claims are readily encountered.

1) *Grieving declines in a steadily decreasing fashion over time.* On the contrary, people may experience very intense upsurges of grief long after the loss occurs. Anniversaries and holidays can bring feelings flooding back. A song or special place may trigger feelings that the survivor

[2]Rando refers to these misconceptions as myths, but in theology, myth has different, more positive connotations.

thought were already resolved. *Chuck LeCompte* (page 67) said hearing the song Jingle Bells or walking into the school gym brought back memories of his son. The grief may intensify as reality sets in and people realize how much they have actually lost. *Tater Ward* (page 56) said his most intense feelings of grief came after the funeral and activity was over and he faced the quiet and absence. Twenty-five and twenty years after her father and brother's deaths, *Doris Hump* (page 61) said, **I'm still grieving. I don't think that's ever going to go away. That's always part of myself.**

2) *If you only express your feelings, that is enough to resolve grieving.* Acknowledging and expressing your feelings is a good beginning and one of the tasks of grieving. *Darlene Young Bear* (page 85) explained that Lakota culture goes so far as to say that if you do not cry, you will get sick. *Richard Charging Eagle* adds, **Laughter and tears - those are the two things that could heal ourselves.** But there are other, more cognitive tasks to be taken care of. Grieving means adjusting to the changed circumstances in the world since the death. Grievers must relearn how to relate and negotiate through those changes. *Iyonne Garreau* (pages 74-75) found that she needed to channel her energy into a career to begin to climb out of the depression she experienced after the death of her infant daughter. Much more than expressing feelings is involved in grieving.

Even when people are able to express their feelings, public displays of emotion are usually considered more of an embarrassment than therapeutic. The ideal in the United States is to avoid making a scene whether at the hospital or place of death, and even at the funeral. Look how well they are holding up is considered a compliment at a funeral. Young people are told to cowboy up and bear the pain silently. Sorrow is judged as morbid, or a sign of instability. We tell ourselves that crying is best done in private. I noticed that parishioners who expressed their emotions in front of others were less likely to get stuck in their grieving than those who tried to act as if nothing were wrong.

3) *You should put the dead person out of your thoughts.* *Doris Hump's* (page 62) story tells of how strongly and righteously she reacted to people trying to convince her of this, when she said, **People talk to you, and**

the time of their death, comforting you with their words. I heard a lot of them say, 'It's gonna take time, but you'll forget, and you're gonna go on with your life.' Yeah, I'm gonna go on with my life, but I'm not gonna forget. I can't forget. The goal is not to *forget* and move on, the goal is to *remember* and move on.

4) *Intensity and length of grieving are indicators of how much you loved someone.* Sometimes victims who have been abused and are filled with rage at what the perpetrator did to them, experience some of the greatest intensity in feelings. Those with a good relationship with the one who died, who perhaps were able to say goodbye and begin to process their feelings with them as they were dying, may have a shorter period of feeling besieged by feelings of intense grief.

5) *Time heals all wounds.* Not automatically. Grieving is hard work. People who work at the social and emotional tasks that need to be taken care of will in time be able to adjust. People who avoid grieving's tasks may remain stuck in the grief no matter how much time passes.

6) *Everything will be OK.* Darlene Young Bear (page 85) forcefully debunked this myth when she exclaimed, **They will come and tell you, Don't cry, Don't cry. It's all right, it'll be OK.'** It's not gonna be OK! Telling people that life is good when it is not, that things will work out when they are not working out, is not honest. People's pain must be acknowledged. Sometimes that pain is overwhelming. While most people can find happiness in life without the deceased, and work through grieving issues, some people's worlds are so disrupted that life never becomes OK again.

SUMMARY

The Whiteheads' method asks us to place the voices of tradition, experience and culture together and listen to their complementing and competing claims. This chapter has provided an overview of the dynamics of grieving from the perspective of the social science and the Christian traditions and brought them into dialogue with Lakota culture and experience. The Lakota experience of traumatic death, multiple loss and conflicted grieving described in chapter two pose particular challenges for grieving which the traditions must address.

The Lakota worldview includes a strong belief in and experience of spirits. Christianity and the social sciences cannot overlook that reality but must find ways to understand and work with people within that framework. Lakota understand that good and bad habits can be formed at a time when grief makes people so vulnerable. But this also makes grieving a time of opportunity for positive life changes.

Christian Scriptures offer people in grief a rich variety of images to address their particular losses. The Order of Catholic Funerals provides a wide range of options to help people ritualize their grief. But cultures like the Lakota had established rituals for grieving long before Christian contact. For inculturation of the gospel to truly happen, adaptation and cosmetic changes in Christian ritual are not enough. Lakota use of music and colors are examples that raise the need for ongoing contextualization.

My ultimate purpose for dialogue around the issue of grieving is pastoral action. This thesis project aims to improve the practice of ministry to people in grief. Chapter four proposes attitudes and strategies toward that end and also suggests ways which the Lakota experience might help others in their grieving.

Chapter Four

Strategies for Pastoral Ministries

WHAT CAN BE LEARNED FROM LAKOTA GRIEVING PRACTICES

One implication of ministering in a culture different from the one you are raised in, is that it ministers new lenses with which to view the world. Mission-in-reverse (Barbour et al. p. 82) is the experience many missionaries have when they immerse themselves in another culture. They set out to teach and serve, but in the process learn and receive. Ministry among the Lakota on Cheyenne River taught me to reexamine the grieving practices I grew up with. I would like to suggest seven ways the Lakota experience of grieving might help others.

1) *Lakota people encourage both those dying and those grieving to directly face death with all its horror.* Doris Hump (page 62) illustrates this attitude when she asserts, **You have to talk about death, or you're gonna run into trouble.** While that can be emotionally draining and hard in the short term, it helps people adjust in the long run. The current societal movements toward hospices and home health care for the dying agree that death should not be sanitized nor shuffled away, but faced openly. When family members see the dying up close, spend time with them and begin to process the reality of their loss, death comes as more of a natural conclusion to life.

2) *Lakota people believe that children should not be kept away from funerals or sheltered from death, but included in all of the practices from start to finish.* Parents will remind children to be good to relatives, because some day they will die. (Brokenleg and Middleton, p. 104). This encourages them to grow in kindness and generosity. But most importantly, it helps them learn from how others how to grieve. Too often in U.S. culture, when children ask about death, they experience adults' discomfort with the topic. They learn that the subject is not a welcome one and keep their questions and concerns to themselves. Lakota elders maintain the importance of regularly talking with children about death and having them be a part of the community which prays for the dead. When the children then experience someone's death, they have an idea of what will be expected of them.

3) *Lakota grieving practices point out that grieving takes time.* Rather than limiting grieving to a short few days and expecting people to quickly

get back to normal, many Lakota people limit their participation in extracurricular activities for a full year. They attend to their families and the changed relationships in light of the death. Time alone does not automatically see people through all the grieving tasks. Grieving takes work. But the work takes time. The cultural expectation of one year of grieving allows people time to attend to those duties before returning to their normal routines.

4) *Giving away all of a loved one's possessions is probably the most distinct aspect of Lakota grieving practices.* Where I grew up, it was more common to see families torn apart by arguing over possessions after someone died. The giveaways seem to help with several psychological tasks. For *Peggy Knife*, (page 70 the giveaway gave her something to look forward to. It moved her out of despair and gave her a reason to keep going. *Darlene Young Bear* (page 86) told of the giveaway's power to symbolically express that the person meant more than any possessions. She went so far as to give away even the bed she shared with her husband. *Debbie Day* (page 60) told of how completing the giveaway brought a feeling of relief.

Giving possessions away also reinforces the reality of the death. The gathering up of the possessions triggers memories of the person's life. Sorting through a lifetime of mementoes allows a unique overview of a personality. Decisions about who is to be honored with the gifts affirm relationships that were significant to the one who died. It also begins to establish new ties between the living. I found this pre-Christian practice prophetically modeling Christianity's golden rule: it is better to give than to receive.

5) *Lakota people emphasize personal presence at funerals, wakes, memorials and other services.* They stress the importance of making the time to participate. The support of a caring community is of great benefit to persons who are grieving. When in doubt about whether to stop by a wake or funeral, I always encourage people to err on the side of attending. Presence says what words alone cannot convey.

6) *Dreams and visions can indicate unfinished business with the dead and prompt a working through of issues.* But beyond the psychological

dimension, there is much about the spiritual world that humanity is at a loss to fully explain. Lakota people's experiences with spirits presents perhaps the greatest challenge for non-Lakota ministers to work with. Experiences that cannot be scientifically or rationally measured should not be dismissed, but used to further personal growth and a working through of the tasks grieving demands.

7) *The dynamics of the Wiping of Tears ceremony model a helpful approach of the community's role in allowing people time to do the needed grieving work.* Grieving strains our relationships and obligations. When grieving we need time to pull back from responsibilities. Lakota people are given a structure that allows them both time to grieve and a ritual closure. After the extended period of grieving, people are ritually welcomed-back into the community and resume their obligations and activities. The public nature of Lakota grieving helps to avoid any privatization of grieving. People are expected to do the spiritual and emotional work that will bring them back into the community.

RECOMMENDATIONS FOR PASTORAL CARE

One of the questions I asked people during the interviews was what advice they might have for someone new who was coming to minister on the reservation. Their responses form the basis of seven principles for ministry. Afterward, I add some recommendations of my own. These conclusions have come through listening to experience, tradition and culture and trying to form approaches that work for ministry in such a situation.

1) **Learn about the culture** *(Suzie Eagle Staff)*. Persons engaged in any kind of ministry should continue learning as much as they can about the culture in which they are working and living. While that may seem an obvious starting point, it needs to be explicitly stated. Successful pastoral care and solid practical theology depend on understanding the context. Learning about the history and culture of any context is enhanced by reading books on the subject. Books are only a beginning. In an oral culture such as the Lakota culture, ministers benefit from seeking out and listening to the stories. Personal histories, such as those central to this pro-

ject, show how those traditions are appropriated and integrated into tribal members' lives. Such stories are a rich source of wisdom and can help the outsider begin to appreciate the intricacies of the culture. Appreciating Lakota culture means concrete things like taking seriously people's experiences of spirits, even if that is foreign to the minister's own worldview.

Lakota language study can assist ministers. It is relatively easy to get by on Cheyenne River without speaking Lakota, because all the tribal members are able to speak English, even though it may not be their language of preference. Even learning the basics like how to say thank you or how to greet people show an attitude of care and respect. But language study also opens the student up to new concepts as language reveals cultural identity. Like any language, Lakota has words for which there are no exact English words or equivalents, because the words are used to express a different way of viewing the world. An understanding of the language is the lens into that worldview. While Western culture uses spirit/soul to describe life after death, learning that Lakota reality uses more words to adequately describe the spiritual world can raise new questions and lead the dialogue in new directions. Another example is how understanding the words people use in relationships leads to a fuller understanding of the Lakota family structure.

Ministers who are not Lakota will always remain outsiders to Lakota Culture. But studying, dialoguing with Lakota spiritual leaders, and carefully observing the practices and ceremonies, can give ministers valid insights. By asking questions that those immersed in the culture take for granted, ministers can encourage Lakota people to seek out a greater understanding of their own history and traditions.

Studying and valuing culture in the Lakota context is made more urgent by the fact that churches in the past have tried to do away with Lakota culture. In 1992, on the five hundredth anniversary of Columbus coming to the Americas, our pastoral team drafted a statement that acknowledged the ways Christianity had harmed Lakota people. We shared that with the parishioners, asked for forgiveness, and pledged to work to heal the wounds. That attempt was met with great appreciation.

Repentance and attempts at reconciliation are sorely needed.

A corollary to principle one: **Take people for what they are . . .**

A lot of outsiders, it makes no difference if they're teachers, doctors, nurses, priests, sisters, when they come here, they want to change everything. They want to change the structure of their home and what they do there, because the house doesn't have anything in there like they **think they should have. When you go into homes, don't judge them by what they have, or don't have in the house. Don't go in there and try to change them.** (*Mona Lawrence*)

Given people's common experiences of spirits, for instance, that might be a specific area to work with people instead of trying to change them. My worldview was opened to new possibilities regarding the spirit world as I respected and honored Lakota people's experience.

2) **As soon as you hear someone has died, go and make contact with the family as soon as possible. Let them know you're available for them.** (*Rosie Roach Avery*). A ministry of availability or presence is demanding. It requires putting away the clock and patiently waiting, allowing the unfolding of whatever needs to happen. Just getting to some of the homes requires driving an hour and a half each way, in good weather! If you share a meal, offer prayers, give people the chance to begin to verbalize their feelings, and share their stories, availability for that one visit may take the better part of the day. But it is extremely important to Lakota parishioners that their ministers reach out to them at this time.

The prayer services held in the home are an ideal time for a ministry of presence. Neighbors and relatives will flow in and out and connections with the extended family are made. Even though the feelings of grief may be intense in this period, the family is more themselves in their own home. Pictures of the deceased on the walls can spark memories and help people to talk about their relationship with the one who died.

If you are connected with a church in any capacity, be prepared to be asked to offer a prayer or some words of wisdom. Prayer in the homes is not just for one denomination, but open to anyone. **It's not [only for] the individual who passed away; we're worried about the ones that are left here** (*Rev. Richard Charging Eagle*).

> I never feel a differing expectation, whether you are a Catholic clergy or brother or religious sister, or any other denomination. People don't distinguish. You are a pastor, regardless of what faith and they welcome you and are very respectful and honored that you can come there and share with them, regardless of denomination. (Interview with *Gary Lantz, SCJ*).

While ministers are expected to pray, there is a great freedom in not being in charge during these spontaneous gatherings. Ritual prayer is obviously an important form of pastoral ministry, with the power to draw people into grieving's tasks. But the gatherings open up the opportunity for another avenue of pastoral ministry, namely hearing people's stories, allowing them to express feelings, hearing how they are trying to make sense of their world given the absence of the deceased.

3) **The Lakota way is to be generous.** (*Darlene Young Bear*) Generosity is one of the four cardinal Lakota virtues and can be expressed as hospitality to visitors. Hospitality goes a long way in helping communicate availability and a sense of caring presence. Knowing how important food and hospitality are, if families come to your office to plan, offering coffee or juice and baked goods is appropriate and helps foster an atmosphere of hospitality. Since people may have come as far as 90 miles from one of the outlying communities, they may need to use the phones or restroom. Treat them as you would a guest arriving after a long road trip before settling into any praying or planning. Always have tissues handy nearby. Ministers shouldn't rush for the tissues at the first sign of tears because that can stifle emotional expression. But a box of tissues within the family's reach communicates that you expect crying and it is acceptable.

4) **Help people plan.** (*Tater Ward*) Tater explained: **This was a whole new experience for us. What needs to be done? We were just running around with our heads in circles, calling and asking people**

what we had to do. Somebody should come up with a list! A factor
n how effective funerals facilitate grieving is the degree of involvement of
he bereaved in the preparation of and/or doing the rites (Smith, p. 91).
Occasionally families are so devastated by a death that they can make
almost no decisions. But most families appreciate the chance to plan and
make choices that express both their beliefs and their relationship with
he deceased. **Ask them how they would go about doing things. Talk with the
family and see what they really want to incorporate into the services.**
(Rosie Roach Avery). Talking through how the services would go and
walking through the rituals provides a chance for both education and dia-
ogue. I could explain, for instance, what the placing of the pall on the cof-
n, or what the use of incense symbolized, and they in turn could explain
heir understanding of when a song or *azilya* was important. It also gave
he opportunity to figure out what kind of liturgical and support ministries
would be called for and to invite people to participate in those.

In making choices about how to ritualize their grieving, families assign
meanings to what they are doing, which facilitates the grieving work that
needs to be done.

Rev. Richard Charging Eagle, a United Church of Christ Minister, asks
he family how they want to mourn. Do they want to enter into a ritual
grieving for the four days, or do they intend to extend the period for the
year? He then goes through what they can expect during that period of
grieving.

A planning mistake that I learned from was in the selection of scripture
readings. My first couple of funerals, I handed people the funeral book-
et which contained all 52 suggested scripture passages and expected
hem to choose. That overwhelmed most people, already overburdened
by too many decisions about the funeral. What I learned was more help-
ul was to ask if they or the deceased had any favorite bible stories, or if
hey could think of any that reminded them of the one who had died.
Some of the scripture passages they chose were not in the funeral lec-
ionary. One family who lost a daughter in a car accident chose Isaiah
43:1-5 which spoke of God's love of them even as they passed through

what felt like raging waters and fire and destruction all around. Another chose Proverbs 31:10-31, the description of the ideal wife, as a way of beginning to create memories of their mother. The scriptures are rich and if the goal is to connect faith with life, grief with Christian hope, then the scriptural possibilities are endless.

Ministers are important resources for helping people access Christian tradition through the scriptures. Some people had no familiarity with scripture, nor any preferences for readings. In those cases, after listening to their recollections about the deceased and the circumstances of death, I offered a few scriptural possibilities and checked to see if any of those resonated with the family.

5) **Work with traditional spiritual leaders.** (*Tom Eagle Staff*) Traditional leaders are willing to talk and work with Christian ministers if asked. They want to be accommodating and work things out for the good of the family. *Tom Eagle Staff* recommends talking over the ceremonies beforehand with any traditional Lakota spiritual leaders the family wants to include. Conflict and confusion can be avoided if the communication is kept open and everyone is kept informed. A few minutes might be all it takes to share what is planned and expected. Most Lakota rituals can be done side by side with Christian ones, though the timing of a ceremony might need to be negotiated. But flexibility and adaptability is a common Lakota characteristic.

Collaboration with members of other Christian traditions is also an ongoing part of ministry on Cheyenne River. Members of Lakota families usually belong to different religious traditions. A general ecumenical sensitivity is not only called for, but generally exists in collaborative practice. Because of the interrelatedness of the small reservation communities anyone's death draws a cross section of the community together. Catholic ministers attending services in another church will be offered the chance to say a few words and the same courtesy is expected in return.

Funeral directors are also a group with whom collaboration is desirable so that the best possible ministry to the grieving is assured.

6) **Check with people after the funeral.** (*Louis Jewett*) Following up after a funeral presents great opportunities to work with people in a way

hat is not possible within the intense period of the funeral rites. People end to receive lots of support in the days immediately following a death. \fterwards, when everyone else goes back to their normal routines, they re stuck with routines that are not as they used to be when their loved ne was alive.

One study of widowed persons showed that while ministers placed reat importance in making themselves available at the time of death and he funeral, the widowed themselves valued the support after the funeral) a greater degree (Rutherford, p. 80 in Boadt). If a minister volunteers) visit later, which everyone says with the best of intentions, but does not)llow through, it can add to the feelings of alienation.

Dropping in for a visit or making a phone call a few weeks or months fter death can be an opportunity if people want to talk about all they have een going through since the death. Anniversaries and holidays may be mes when contact can be especially appreciated. The task of those who are for people in grief, is to help them find the language to deepen their wareness of the pain they are experiencing. (Anderson, 1993, p. 381). \sking how people are doing rather than politely avoiding the subject is enerally appreciated.

There are also times when grieving people want and need to be left lone. Their grieving is not helped by trying to rush them into talking efore they are ready. A reluctance to talk need not signal denial. A certain amount of withdrawal is necessary for important internal work that rieving demands. When people are ready to talk the minister needs to e prepared to stay and listen for a while. Listening also requires pastoral aregivers to be comfortable with silence.

Often ongoing, regularly scheduled appointments do not work as well s home visits and the chance to tell the entire story in one sitting. In a ural setting, one of the best forums is sitting around the kitchen table with he person or the entire family in their home. It is more important to listen to a person and a community than to try to solve their problems, and especially to continue to do so, after the funeral (Dombeck p. 63).

7) **Take into account what the kids or the grandchildren are feeling.** (*Eileen Peacock*) One of the great temptations at the time of death

139

is to devote our pastoral attention to very few people - that is, to those who are closest to the deceased. While these people certainly deserve such attention, they are only part of the picture. (Rutherford, p. 11)

Ministry to the grieving can be biased toward the adults. The husband or wife, or an adult child will usually get more attention than a school aged child or grandchild. One of the High School Counselors, described students who come to see her:

> **Sometimes I think when they come into the office they just cry by themselves - a grief that they have just for themselves. Because it's just them and I'm listening to them. It's not mom crying too. They want someone to just deal with them, for only just them. At the funeral they might be crying because their mom is hurting so bad, or because their best friend is hurting so bad. When they come into the office and they cry by themselves, it's like this is all mine now. This is all MY pain now. I can cry in front of Mrs. Peacock and she'll listen to me, and it'll just be me! That death may be affecting them in a very profound way, those younger kids, and we don't pay enough attention to them when they grieve.** (*Eileen Peacock*).

When an elder dies, those in helping professions may be so focused on their grown children, that they do not always take into account what others, especially the younger members of the family, are feeling. The social sciences urge pastoral care workers to look at the disruptions a death causes throughout the entire family system.

Eileen Peacock also warned that many of the young people she sees do not have a solid grounding in either Christian or Lakota spirituality, which leaves them with fewer resources to draw upon during times of death and tragedy. That may necessitate more outreach on pastoral ministers' part to help them to feel included and supported during the church rituals.

PASTORAL REFLECTIONS

In addition to what Lakota parishioners expect from ministers, I have my own principles for ministry to the grieving.

1) *Listen to the story.* Sometime before the funeral, I begin to hear the grievers' stories about the deceased person's life and how the death was affecting them. Sometimes that meant listening to pain and despair while feeling helpless to do anything, but often people need somebody to listen more than anything. Telling the story begins the process of the making of memories, which is an essential grieving task. Listening to the story of a person from another culture challenged me to enter into their worldview and see life from a new perspective.

Many opportunities exist for story telling. The wake, with the meal and community gathered, is a natural forum. After planning services with the family or while visiting the home, one could ask, What are some of your memories of (name)? Listening to the story can be a way of support offered by anyone in the community, particularly friends and neighbors. I remember when . . . can begin a whole chain of memories that allows grievers the freedom to laugh and cry and remember.

A fringe benefit for a minister who will preach at the wake or funeral, is that hearing stories helps them understand what kind of questions the death has raised and what the grieving family is asking of God as they try to make meaning of the event. This is helpful in being able to make connections between faith and life. While some family members may choose to stay at the wake all night, ministers are not expected to. People understand that ministers have other responsibilities. But it is good pastoral practice to hang around after the formal prayers of the wake are finished and spend time with people as they are eating and visiting.

2) *Remember the issues that complicate grieving.* Where the death raises guilt and anger, it is important to give people the opportunity to process those feelings. One attempt our pastoral team made was to offer the sacrament of reconciliation during the wakes, to allow people who realized ways they had hurt the deceased to bring that to prayer. People who have been hurt by the deceased likewise can be helped by a forum where it is safe to talk about how that has affected them, especially if their cultural ways do not always encourage the expression of anger and ill

feelings. These issues can be kept in mind as part of follow up and ongoing pastoral care.

Long term abuse is best dealt with by trained professionals in a long term therapeutic relationship with the individual. But there is limited availability for that on the reservation. The more trust ministers gain from people, the more stories of abuse come forward and demand whatever kinds of pastoral response are possible. Abuse issues seem best dealt with in the times of follow up visits, when the immediacy of the emotional reactions has been given some time to sink in.

Regarding multiple loss, in a small town atmosphere, ministers are often aware of other deaths that are affecting grievers. In ongoing pastoral care though, it can be helpful to ask if there are other deaths people are still grieving.

3) *Grief Ministry must be part of ongoing parish ministry.* Funerals should not be the only times in the life of a parish where grieving is dealt with. Regular parish liturgies are important rehearsals for us, so that when death comes it will not be a complete stranger. It will rather be something of the Church (Rutherford, p. 12). There is a need for catechesis in parishes regarding funeral rites, but also to lead the community to a deeper appreciation of its role in the ministry of consolation and to a fuller understanding of the significance of the death of a fellow Christian. (OCF #9). OCF calls for the development of lay leadership for funerals and for grief ministry in general.

There are many times the Sunday lectionary raises issues of death and end times which provide excellent opportunities for focusing on the Christian response in the face of death and grieving. Take home sheets might be passed out in conjunction with such a homily. Support groups might be developed, or a weekend retreat to give those grieving a chance to process what has happened. Anniversaries of deaths can be remembered in the bulletin. In November, in connection with the feasts of All Saints and All Souls, we gathered and mentioned aloud the names of the deceased during the masses. There are countless ways to make the community aware of how the grieving can be ministered to.

Encouraging full and active participation by the assembly can be a pastoral challenge in an area where, for a large number of people, funerals are their primary, or only, experience of church. Funerals are often occasions for outreach to the unchurched and to the larger community. If Catholic worship is not familiar to many in the assembly, extra care needs to be taken to help people feel welcome. Regular church goers can be encouraged to extend hospitality. Funeral booklets or simple instructions can help people have a better sense of what is expected of them.

Lakota culture encourages people to help with any chores and tasks required by the family, cleaning, cooking, running errands. That can extend to the church as well, where people are very willing to help if asked to move chairs, act as ushers, help set up tables for a meal. People like to be able to contribute. Labor is a ritual action that can show care for the deceased.

CONCLUSION

In the Lakota way, before someone speaks, no toastmaster reads off their degrees or accomplishments. The speaker introduces him or herself. They *hanbloglaka* - tell of their vision and about their experiences. In telling a personal history, it gives the listener a definite context with which to judge the biases, the limitations and the integrity of what the speaker says. I realize that I have given my interpretation of the grieving practices of a particular group of Lakota Catholics and from that, I have attempted to point out some directions for ministry. Others who bring a fuller understanding of the cultures and traditions involved, including the experience of grieving, will draw other conclusions. I offer this thesis project not as a conclusion, but as a beginning of an ongoing dialogue around this issue. I hope to encourage members of this culture, which is both Lakota and Christian, to find an integration which draws on the resources of both these rich traditions, and helps people through their grieving.

Appendices

Appendices

Appendix One

Cheyenne River Sioux Reservation
(1990 Census statistics)

Enrolled members	9841
Tribal Members living on Reservation	5092
Median age	19.2 years

Education

Over 25 years of age & High School Graduate	60.8%
Over 25 years of age & Bachelor's Degree	.7%

Family & Poverty

< 18 years old & living with two parents	42.3%
Individuals living below poverty line	59.7%
< 18 years old, living below poverty line	64.9%
Families living below poverty line	57.2%

Employment

> 16 years old & in labor force	54.3%
Unemployed	27.9%
(South Dakota Statewide unemployment)	4.3%
% of workers employed by government	59.3%
% manufacturing jobs	00.4%

Appendix One

Cheyenne River Sioux Reservation

(1990 Census statistics)

	Per capita income	Median family income
All U.S	$14,420	$35,225
All U.S rural	$12,408	$31,463
South Dakota	$10,661	$27,602
Cheyenne River	$ 4,077	$10,870

Per Capita Income

All Dewey County	$6,515
All Ziebach County	$6,312
Dewey County American Indian	$4,344
Ziebach County American Indian	$3,382

American Indian Households without:

	(By County)	
	Dewey	Ziebach
Vehicle	24%	32%
Telephone	44%	60%
Plumbing	7%	22%

Appendix Two: Deaths per 100,000 Population

Cause of Death	Years	All USA Races	All Indian Health Service Areas	Cheyenne River Sioux Reservation
Malignant Neoplasms	1989-1991	135	94.5	195.7
	1990-1992	134.5	96.1	217.9
Pnemonia / Flu	1989-1991	14	20.5	18.9
	1990-1992	13.4	19.7	28.9
Suicide	1989-1991	11.5	16.5	41.7
	1990-1992	11.4	16.2	45
Unintentional Injuries	1989-1991	37	86	145.7
	1990-1992	31	83.2	111.1
Motor Vehicle Accidents	1989-1991	18.8	48.3	74.1
	1990-1992	17	47.5	70.6
Other Accidents	1989-1991	18.2	37.6	71.5
	1990-1992	13.9	37.6	40.5

Appendix Two: Deaths per 100,000 population

Cause of Death	Years[1]	USA All Races	All Indian Health Service Areas	Cheyenne River Sioux Reservation
Alcoholism	1989-1991	7.1	37.6	57.8
	1990-1992	6.8	37.2	56.5
Cerebrovascular Disease	1989-1991	27.7	25.2	25.7
	1990-1992	26.8	24.9	36.1
Chronic Liver Disease	1989-1991	8.6	30.3	47.8
	1990-1992	8.3	29.5	64.8
Chronic Obstructive Pulmonary Disease	1989-1991	19.7	13.8	42.2
	1990-1992	20.1	13.5	41.3
Mellitus	1989-1991	11.7	29.7	36.4
	1990-1992	11.8	30	46.1
Heart Disease	1989-1991	152	132.1	214.8
	1990-1992	148.2	131.3	187.5
Homicide	1989-1991	10.2	15.3	18.7
	1990-1992	10.9	14.6	9.7

[1]Averages taken from 3-year rates provide more accurate reflection of the rea in areas of small population where the rates would swing more widely from year to year.

Cheyenne River Leading Rates of Years of Potential Life Lost Before Age 65 (per 10,000 Population)

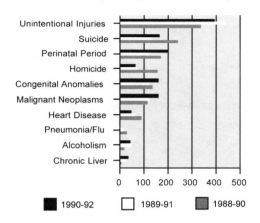

Age of Death

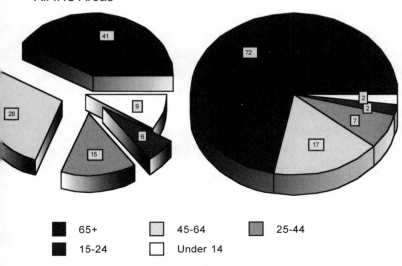

1990-1992 Aberdeen
All IHS Areas

1991 All U.S.

Appendix Five:

GLOSSARY of Lakota terms used

aya (wo'aya) habit.

azilya incensing, smudging, with sage, sweet grass or cedar.

cannunpa sacred pipe

cannumpa yuha wocekiye the Pipe Ceremony.

hanbloglaka tell of a vision

hokahe (Hoka hey) welcome, come on in (urges action)

hunkayapi Making of Relatives ceremony

Ic'ilowan the death song

inipi sweat bath

lala grandfather

maya winuhcala Ghost Woman, Owl Woman

nagi spirit

ni (niya) breath, life

onuniya u forever

sicun that aspect of soul which is immortal

Tate the wind

tipi tent, home

tiyospaye the extended family system

tunkasila Grandfather. Also used to name God

wakan holy

wakanheja child

wakan tanka Great Spirit, Great Mystery, God

wanagi ghosts

wanagi chanku, wanagi tacanku Ghost path, spirit's path

wanagi gluhapi ghost keeping ceremony

wanagi kte (ghost kills) a stroke

wanagi makoce Ghost country

wanagiyate iyaya gone to the spirit land

wasna traditional food of dried buffalo meat, tallow, and mashed chokeche

wateca food that is taken home after a feed

wicat olowan mourning song

wihpeyapi giveaway, to dispose of things

wocekiye wicasa men of prayer

wojapi fruit and starch pudding

Bibliography

Abrogast, Doyle, 1995: <u>Wounded Warriors - A Time For Healing</u>, Omaha NE, Little Turtle Publications.

Amiotte, Arthur,: "Our Other Selves: The Lakota Dream Experience." <u>Parabola</u> 7(2):26-32.

Anderson, Herbert, 1984: <u>The Family and Pastoral Care</u> Philadelphia PA, Fortress Press.

Anderson, Herbert, 1993: What Consoles? <u>Sewanee Theological Review</u>: 36:3, pp. 374-384.

Aries, Philippe, 1974: <u>Western Attitudes Toward Death From the Middle Ages To the Present</u>, Baltimore John Hopkins Press.

Attig, Thomas, 1996: <u>How We Grieve: Relearning the World</u> New York, Oxford University Press.

Attneave, Carolyn, 1982: American Indians and Alaska Native Families: Emigrants in Their Own Homeland in <u>Ethnicity and Family Therapy</u>, Ed. McGoldrick, Pearce & Giordano, Guilford Press New York 55-83.

Bane, J. Donald, et al. Ed., 1975: <u>Death and Ministry - Pastoral Care of the Dying and the Bereaved</u> New York, Seabury Press.

Barbour, Claude Marie, Billman, Kathleen, DesJarlait, Peggy, and Doidge, Eleanor, 1994: Ministry on the Boundaries, in <u>Beyond Theological Tourism: mentoring as a grassroots approach to theological education</u>, editors Thistlewaite, Susan B. and Cairus, George F., Maryknoll New York, Orbis.

Barclay, William, 1975: <u>The Gospel of John Vol 2</u> Philadelphia, The Westminster Press.

Becker, Ernest, 1973: <u>The Denial of Death</u>, New York, The Free Press.

Bevans, Stephen, SVD, 1992: <u>Models of Contextual Theology</u>, Maryknoll NY, Orbis Press.

Black Bear, Ben, Jr., 1990: Distinctions exist between Lakota, Christian burial rites <u>West River Catholic</u>, Rapid City, SD, October 1990, 4B.

Black Bear, Ben Sr. and Theisz, R.D., 1984: <u>Songs and Dances of the Lakota</u>, Aberdeen, SD, North Plains Press.

Blankenhorn, David, 1995: Fatherless America: Confronting our Most Urgent Social Problem, New York, BasicBooks.

Blasingame, Ike, 1964: Dakota Cowboy: My Life in the Old Days, Lincoln, University of Nebraska Press.

Boadt, Lawrence, C.S.P., Dombeck, Mary and Rutherford, H. Richard, C.S.C., 1988: Rites of Death and Dying Collegeville, MN, The Liturgical Press.

Brokenleg, Martin, and Middleton, David, 1993: Native Americans: Adapting, Yet Retaining in Ethnic Variations in Dying Death and Greif: Diversity in Universality Washington, Taylor and Francis, pp. 101-112.

Brown, Dee, 1991: Bury My Heart at Wounded Knee New York, Henry Holt and Company.

Brown, Joseph Epes, 1953: The Sacred Pipe: Black Elk's Account of the Seven Rites of the Oglala Sioux Norman, OK, University of Oklahoma Press.

Browning, Don S., 1991: A Fundamental Practical Theology, Minneapolis, Fortress Press.

Bruggemann, Walter, 1979: Covenanting as Human Vocation, Interpretation, 33:2, April.

Buechel, Eugene, S.J., 1983: Dictionary - Oie Wowapi Wan of Teton Sioux, Pine Ridge, SD, Red Cloud Indian School.

Bureau of Indian Affairs, 1951: Location and Census of Indian Cemeteries: Cheyenne River Indian Reservation, South Dakota. Report #120 Missouri River Basin Investigations, BIA, Billings, Montana, June 20, 1951.

Burrows, William R., Editor, 1993: Redemption and Dialogue: Reading Redemptoris Missio and Dialogue and Proclamation, Maryknoll, NY, Orbis.

Churchill, Larry R., 1979: The Human Experience of Dying: The Moral Primacy of Stories Over Stages, Soundings #62, 24-37

Congregation For Divine Worship, 1975: General Instruction of the Roman Missal, Catholic Book Publishing Co. New York.

Congregation for Divine Worship and Discipline of the Sacraments, 1994:

The Roman Liturgy and Inculturation Washington DC, United States Catholic Conference.

Crow Dog, Mary, 1990: Lakota Woman, New York, Harper.

Deloria, Vine, Jr., 1974: The Indian Affair 1974, New York, Friendship Press.

DeMallie, Raymond J. & Parks, Douglas R.,1987: Sioux Indian Religion Norman, OK, University of Oklahoma Press.

Eastman, Charles, 1980: The Soul of The Indian: an Interpretation, Lincoln, University of Nebraska Press.

Economic Development Administration, 1996: American Indian Reservations and Trust Areas Ed. Tiller, Veronica E. Velarde, U.S. Department of Commerce, Albuquerque, NM.

Engelhardt, H. Tristram, 1975: Medicine and the Naturalness of Death: The Counsels of Finitude Hastings Center Report #5, Hastings

Fergus, Charles, 1991: Shadow Catcher, New York, Soho.

Fire, John and Erdos, Richard, 1994: Lame Deer: Seeker of Visions, New York, Washington Square Press.

Flannery, Austin, Editor, 1975: Vatican Council II: The Conciliar and Post Conciliar Documents, Northport, NY, Costello Publishing Company.

Flannery, Austin, Editor, 1982: Vatican Council II: More Post Conciliar Documents, Collegeville, MN, The Liturgical Press.

Goble, Paul, 1993: Beyond the Ridge Aladdin Books, New York.

Groome, Thomas, 1991: Sharing Faith: A Comprehensive Approach to Religious Education & Pastoral Ministry San Francisco, Harper.

Hackman, John, SCJ, 1934: Pagan Sioux Custom Made Christian in The Mission Call, Vol VI Number 1, January-February 11.

Hassrick, Royal B., 1964: The Sioux, Norman, OK, University of Oklahoma Press.

Hatcher, John, SJ et al., 1994 - 1996: Diocese of Rapid City Lakota

Inculturation Task Force, Unpublished summaries, Rapid City, South Dakota.

Hoehner, Bernard A., 1996: Going Home Parobola, Vol XXI #2, May, 87-88.

Holler, Clyde, 1984: Lakota Religion and Tragedy: the Theology of Black Elk Speaks, Journal of the American Academy of Religion, 52: (no.1) 19-45.

Holler, Clyde, 1995: Black Elk's Religion: The Sun Dance and Lakota Catholicism, Syracuse, New York, Syracuse University Press.

Huntington, Richard, and Metcalf, Peter, 1979: Celebrations of Death: The Anthropology of Mortuary Ritual, Birmingham, New York, Cambridge University Press.

International Commission on English in the Liturgy, 1982: Pastoral Care of the Sick, Collegeville, MN, The Liturgical Press.

International Commission on English in the Liturgy, 1989: Order of Christian Funerals, Chicago, IL, Liturgical Training Publications.

John Paul II, 1985: Slavorum Apostoli, in Documentation Catholique, June 2.

Kramer, Kenneth, 1988: The Sacred Art of Dying: How World Religions Understand Death Mahwah, NJ, Paulist Press.

Kreig, Robert, 1984: The Funeral Homily: A Theological Dimension, Worship 58:3, 232 - 239

Kübler-Ross, Elisabeth, 1969: On Death and Dying, New York, Macmillian.

Lewis, Thomas H., 1990: The Medicine Men: Oglala Sioux Ceremony and Healing Lincoln, University of Nebraska Press.

Littlewood, Jane, 1992: Aspects of Grief - Bereavement in Adult Life New York, Tavistock/Routledge.

Madigan, Shawn, 1988: Spirituality Rooted in Liturgy, Washington DC, Pastoral Press.

McGaa, Ed (Eagle Man), 1990: Mother Earth Spirituality: Native American Paths to Healing Ourselves and Our World Harper, San Francisco.

McLaughlin, Marie, 1990: <u>Myths and Legends of the Sioux</u> University of Nebraska Press, Lincoln.

Mesteth, Wilmer, Standing Elk, Darrell, & Swift Hawk, Phyllis, 1996: Declaration of War Against Exploiters of Lakota Spirituality unpublished paper

Miller, Robert J, and Hrycyniak, Stephen J, 1996: <u>Griefquest</u>, One Caring Place, Abbey Press, St. Meinrad, IN.

Mitchell, Kenneth R., and Anderson, Herbert, 1983: <u>All Our Losses, All Our Griefs</u> Philadelphia, PA, Westminster Press.

Native American Development Corporation (not dated): Post Traumatic Stress: What Some Indain Youth and Vietnam Veterans Have in Common, Washington DC, NADC

Neihardt, John G., 1972: <u>Black Elk Speaks</u> USA, Washington Square Press.

Nurge, Ethel, Editor, 1970: <u>The Modern Sioux</u> Lincoln, Nebraska, University of Nebraska Press.

Peelman, Achiel, 1995: <u>Christ Is A Native American</u> Montmagny, Quebec, Marquis.

Pinger, George, SCJ, 1939: Indian Memorial Day, in <u>The Mission Call</u>, Vol I Number 4, July-August, 102

Poling, James Newton, 1991: <u>The Abuse of Power: A Theological Problem</u>, Nashville, TN, Abingdon Press.

Powers, Marla N., 1986: <u>Oglala Women</u>, Chicago, University of Chicago Press.

Powers, William K., 1975: <u>Oglala Religion</u>, Lincoln, University of Nebraska Press.

Powers, William K., 1986: <u>Sacred Language: The Nature of Supernatural Discourse in Lakota</u>, University of Oklahoma Press, Norman, OK.

Ramshaw, Elaine, 1987: <u>Ritual and Pastoral Care</u> Philadelphia PA, Fortress Press.

Rando, Therese, 1993: <u>Treatment of Complicated Mourning</u> Champaign IL, Research Press.

Reynolds, Frank E., and Waugh, Earle H., Editors, 1977: <u>Religiou Encounters With Death: Insights from the History and Anthropology Religions</u> University Park, PA, The Pennsylvania State University Press

Riggs, Stephen Return, 1893: <u>Dakota Grammar, Texts and Ethnograph</u> U.S. Government Printing Office, Washington.

Rosenblatt, Paul C., Walsh, R. Patricia, and Jackson, Douglas A., 1970 <u>Grief and Mourning in Cross Cultural Perspective</u> Washington, Huma Relations Area Files Press.

Rutherford, H. Richard, C.S.C., 1990: <u>The Order of Christian Funerals: A Invitation To Pastoral Care</u> The Liturgical Press, Collegeville, MN.

St. Pierre, Mark, 1991: <u>Madonna Swan: A Lakota Woman's Story</u> Norman OK, University of Oklahoma Press.

Schreiter, Robert J., C.P.P.S, 1995 <u>Constructing Local Theologie</u> Maryknoll, New York, Orbis Books.

SEDOS, *Authentic Dialogue Today,* in Jenkinson, William and O'Sulliva Helene, Editors, 1991: <u>Trends in Mission: Toward the Millenium: Essays Celebration of twenty-five years of SEDOS</u> Maryknoll, NY, Orbis, pp. 28 291

Senior, Donald C.P., 1979: <u>Loving and Dying: A Commentary on th Lectionary Texts for Weddings and Funerals</u>, Kansas City, Missour Celebration Books.

Simcoe, Mary Ann, Editor, 1985: <u>The Liturgy Documents - A Paris Resource</u>, Chicago, Liturgy Training Publications.

Smith, Margaret, S.G.S., 1994: <u>The Order of Christian Funerals: Proces of Remembering and Hoping</u> Chicago, IL, Catholic Theological Union.

Smolarski, Dennis C., 1997: Is a Eulogy Ever Permitted at a Funeral <u>Liturgy 90</u>, Volume 28 No. 2, February - March 1997, LTP Chicago, IL.

Speyer, Joseph, SCJ, 1931: The Burial Services in Use Among th Indians in <u>The Mission Call</u> - Priests of the Sacred Heart, Publicatic Office, Champaign, IL, Vol 3 #3, May-June, 86-88 pradley, James P., 1979: The Ethnographic Interview Orlando, FL, Harcourt Brace Jovanovich College Publishers.

prang, Ginny, and McNeil, John, 1995: The Many Faces of Bereavement: The Nature and Treatment of Natural, Traumatic and Stigmatized Grief New York, Brunner/Mazel Publishers.

Starkloff, Carl F., SJ 1994: The Problem of Syncretism in the Search for Inculturation Mission 1, 1994, 75-94

Steinmetz, Paul B., 1980: Pipe, Bible and Peyote Among the Oglala Lakota: a study in religious identity, Stockholm, Almqvist & Wiksell International

Steinmetz, Paul B., 1984: Meditations with Native Americans: Lakota Spirituality, Santa Fe, NM, Bear.

Steltenkamp, Michael F., 1993: Black Elk: Holy Man of the Oglala, University of Oklahoma Press, Norman.

Steltenkamp, Michael F., 1982: The Sacred Vision: Native American Religion and its Practice Today, New York, Paulist Press.

Stolzman, William, S.J., 1986: The Pipe and Christ Chamberlain, SD, Tipi Press.

Tinker, George E., 1993: Missionary Conquest: The Gospel and Native American Cultural Genocide Minneapolis, Minnesota, Augsburg Fortress.

Toynbee, Arnold, and others, 1969: Man's Concern With Death New York, McGraw Hill.

U. S. Army Engineer District, 1965: Final Report: Stage II Cemetery Relocations Oahe Dam and Reservoir Corps of Engineers, Omaha.

U. S. Army Engineer District, 1968: Final Report: Stage IV Cemetery Relocations Oahe Dam and Reservoir Corps of Engineers, Omaha, 1968.

United States Catholic Conference, 1977: Statement of U.S. Catholic Bishops on American Indians, USCC Publications, Washington D.C.

United States Catholic Conference, 1980: Cultural Pluralism in the United States USCC Publications, Washington D.C.

United States Department of Commerce, 1993: <u>1990 Census o</u>
<u>Population</u>, Bureau of the Census, Washington DC.
——- Social and Economic Characteristics, 1993
——- General Population Characteristics, 1993
——- Population and Housing Characteristics, 1993

U.S. Department of Health and Human Services, 1996a: <u>Mortality Chart</u>
Aberdeen Area Indian Health Service, Public Health Service, March 1996
Office of Planning & Legislation, Aberdeen, South Dakota.

U.S. Department of Health and Human Services, 1996b: <u>Years c</u>
<u>Potential Life Lost</u> Aberdeen Area Indian Health Service, Public Health
Service, March 1996, Office of Planning & Legislation, Aberdeen, South
Dakota.

U.S. Department of Health and Human Services, 1996c: <u>Regiona</u>
<u>Differences in Indian Health 1996</u>, Indian Health Services, Rockville, MD

Utley, Robert M., 1994: <u>The Lance and the Shield: The Life and Times c</u>
<u>Sitting Bull</u>, New York, Ballantine Books.

Walker, James R., and edited by DeMallie, Raymond, 1982: <u>Lakota</u>
<u>Society</u>, Lincoln, NE, University of Nebraska Press.

Walker, James R., and edited by Jahner, Elaine, 1983: <u>Lakota Myth</u>
Lincoln, NE, University of Nebraska Press.

Walker, James R., and edited by Jahner, Elaine, and DeMallie, Raymond
1991: <u>Lakota Belief and Ritual</u>, Lincoln, NE, University of Nebraska Press

Walsh, Froma, and McGoldrick, Monica, 1991: <u>Living Beyond Loss: Deat</u>
<u>In The Family</u>, New York, W. W. Norton.

Whitehead, James and Evelyn, 1995: <u>Method in Ministry: Theologica</u>
<u>Reflection and Christian Ministry</u> Kansas City, Missouri, Sheed & Ward.

Young Bear, Sever and Theisz, R.D., 1994: <u>Standing In The Light: /</u>
<u>Lakota Way of Seeing</u>, Lincoln, NE, University of Nebraska Press.

Zeilinger, Ron, 1990: <u>Sacred Ground: Reflections on Lakota Spiritualit</u>
<u>and the Gospel</u> Chamberlain, SD, Tipi Press.